The
Relentless
Tenderness
of Jesus

Other books by Brennan Manning:

Above All
Abba's Child
The Boy Who Cried Abba: A Parable of Trust and Acceptance
A Glimpse of Jesus: Stranger to Self-Hatred
Journey of the Prodigal: A Journey of Sin and Redemption
Posers, Fakers, and Wannabes: Unmasking the Real You
The Rabbi's Heartbeat
Ruthless Trust: The Way of the Ragamuffin
The Ragamuffin Gospel
Reflections for Ragamuffins: A Daily Devotional
Signature of Jesus
The Wisdom of Tenderness

The Relentless Tenderness of Jesus

Brennan Manning

Revell

Grand Rapids, Michigan

© 1986, 2004 by Brennan Manning

Published by Revell
a division of Baker Book House Company
P.O. Box 6287, Grand Rapids, MI 49516-6287

Previously published in 1986 under the title *Lion and Lamb* by Chosen Books

Printed in the United States of America

Sixth printing, March 2009

Library of Congress Cataloging-in-Publication Data
Manning, Brennan.
    The relentless tenderness of Jesus / Brennan Manning.
        p.   cm.
    Rev. ed. of : Lion and lamb. c1986.
    Includes bibliographical references.
    ISBN 0-8007-9339-0 (pbk.)
    1. God—Love. 2. Christian life. I. Manning, Brennan. Lion and lamb. II. Title.
    BT140.M36 2004
    231'.6—dc22   2003020891

For Pete and Lois Kelley/Smith, whose refusal to quit has charged the old cliché "Hang in there" with new meaning, humor and hope.

For I will be like a lion to Ephraim,
   like a great lion to Judah.
I will tear them to pieces and go away;
   I will carry them off, with no one to rescue them.
. . . And they will seek my face.

Hosea 5:14–15

Worthy is the Lamb, who was slain,
to receive power and wealth and wisdom and strength
and honor and glory and praise!

Revelation 5:12

Contents

Foreword

wo personal encounters with Brennan have especially marked my life.

The first came after my request for spiritual direction. A spirit of bitterness had taken root in my heart and I couldn't shake it. As I confessed the ugly details, Brennan teared up. *Oh, great!* I thought to myself. *Something I said triggered some of Brennan's mess, and now I've got to take care of him.*

As I was adding pride and noble self-pity to my already present bitterness, Brennan said quietly, "Larry, every time I'm with you, I'm so drawn to Jesus."

I couldn't have been more surprised. "Why?" I asked.

"Because you hate anything that gets in between you and Abba."

I sang at the top of my lungs in my car all the way home. Someone had seen me with the eyes of redeeming and hopeful love. *So that's the gospel!* I remember thinking to myself.

The second encounter took place on the balcony of a ninth-floor hotel room. Brennan and I had just finished speaking to a pastors' convention, and we were enjoying a brief moment of quiet before leaving for the airport.

"Where to next?" I asked innocently.

"I start a seven-day silent retreat tomorrow," he replied. "I'm not leading it, I'm taking it."

"Brennan, help me here. I know you're into that sort of thing. How are you different after getting away for a week with just you and the Lord?"

Without conscious intent (I think), Brennan gently cut through my American pragmatism when he answered, "I don't know what it does for me. I've never thought much about that. I just figure God likes it when I show up."

I walked away from that encounter more thirsty to experience the Father's fondness for me.

Reading *The Relentless Tenderness of Jesus* has been a third encounter, but, like the two I've mentioned, not really an encounter with Brennan but with God.

"A mystic is a person whose life is ruled by thirst." That's in chapter 12.

I began reading this book a couple of hours ago and just now finished. It came at a good time. I have set this week aside as a sort of personal retreat. My journey has taken me recently into the desert. It's hot and I'm thirsty. But all I've been able to see is burning sand stretching out all the way to the horizon. With no water in sight, thirst had nearly given way to resignation. I've been trying to call it trust.

I've been here before. There's a pattern. When I put down my shovel, when I quit trying to figure out what I must do to find water, a well seems to bubble up.

This time the Spirit used Brennan's book. I can sense resignation yielding to renewed thirst, and hope. As I read these honest, grace-saturated, humbly iconoclastic, distinctly un-sugar-coated but still somehow gentle words, I could taste familiar water, living water that only people who are thirsty for life can enjoy.

Radical Christianity. The real thing. An upending encounter with Jesus that changes everything. Experiencing His love. Letting the Lion tear away every false hope. Riding the Lamb all the way home. That's what this book is all about. Read it—and hope again!

Dr. Larry Crabb

A Word Before

On the eve of His death, Jesus prayed to the Father: "that you love them as you loved me . . . so that your love for me may live in them" (John 17:23, 26 NAB). The same verses in *The Message* read: "that you've sent me and loved them in the same way you've loved me . . . so that your love for me might be in them exactly as I am."

This conjoined passage bends the mind, stuns the heart and beggars speech. It is the cause of ecstatic utterance among the saints, the source of spiritual intoxication among the mystics and, along with the incarnation, the most extraordinary demand ever made on Christian faith. It simply seems incredible.

God loves you just as much as He loves His Son, Jesus Christ.

This is what Scripture says without nuance and with utter precision. Of course, the radical leftists and the right-wing extremists, with their one-note agendas, vociferously protest, because neither can live with biblical clarity. On the right, words without nuance terrify; on the left, there must be nuance for nitpicking. The mavens of the media on both sides are apoplectic, hurling accusations of fundamentalism from the left and lunatic liberalism from the right.

Neither side knows the God revealed by and in Jesus Christ. The divide between human beings and God is nowhere more apparent than here. You may like your spouse 90 percent, a colleague at work 50 percent and your attorney 20 percent. If you assume that God divides His affection with 100 percent for Jesus, 70 percent for Mother Teresa and 2 percent for you, you are thinking not of God but of yourself. As Peter van Breeman notes, "We *have* love, but God *is* love." Love is not one of many activities that God pursues. It is His entire being.

The psalmist writes, "Pause awhile, and know that I am God" (46:10 JB). I favor the Jerusalem Bible translation because it takes time for me to be still, to come to that place of inner quiet. Stillness is more than silence and it is beyond solitude. Interior stillness is too deep for words. Unhampered by self-consciousness, our attention is focused entirely on God and His love. In this sacred now, we immediately understand that God cannot measure His love, giving 100 percent to Jesus and a tiny fraction to us. When Catherine of Siena, a dynamic contemplative in action, was asked to describe the God of her personal experience, she cried, "He is *pazzo d'amore, ebro d'amore*"—crazed with love, drunk with love. Yet her words are feeble and inadequate, as are all human words, because Mystery is spoiled by a word.

"Concepts create idols," wrote Gregory of Nyssa. "Only wonder understands anything." The eminent German theologian Karl Rahner, who died in 1985, wrote: "Some things are understood not by grasping but by allowing oneself to be grasped." As you read these pages, I pray that you allow yourself to be grasped, and that you "pause awhile" and let yourself be loved in your brokenness.

Reaping the Blessings of the Book

An Internal Guide for Group Study

There are two ways to read a book, and I have used both. The first way is an external reading in order to gather information that I will employ to write a sermon, to lead a discussion, to quote in a book I am writing, to support my position in a debate or to determine whether this particular book would be helpful to a seeker or a struggling friend.

The second way is an internal reading in order to experience the content and to personalize the God described within its pages. This approach requires that I read slowly, frequently pause to meditate on the paragraph just read and sometimes read the entire book a second time. I seek transformation more than information, and the time devoted to the task is soaked in prayer.

I have learned through personal experience that sharing insights and reflections with a small group in a prayerful setting is an invaluable help. When circumstances do not allow for such a gathering, the Holy Spirit will not leave you orphan as you study. (I cannot say alone, for as theologian Tad Dunne comments, "Spiritual maturity is giving up the illusion that I can ever be alone.")

EXPERIENCING
JESUS

CHAPTER 1

Healing Our Image of God and Ourselves

Over the past fifteen years my ministry has been identified, more than anything else, with healing our image of God. Teachings on the unconditional love of God, Abba, Father, have aimed at dispelling illusions and myths and helping people to experience the God of Jesus Christ. This, I believe, is the main business of religion. Religion is a matter not of learning how to think about God but of actually encountering Him.

Losing our illusions is painful because illusions are the stuff we live by. The Spirit of God is the great unmasker of illusions, the great destroyer of icons and idols. God's love for us is so great that He does not permit us to harbor false images, no matter how attached we are to them. God strips those falsehoods from us no matter

17

how naked it may make us, because it is better to live naked in truth than closed in fantasy.

Still, there is a chronic temptation to reduce God to human dimensions, to express Him in manageable ideas. Human reason seeks to understand, to reduce everything to its own terms. But God is God. He is more than a superhuman being with an intellect keener than ours and a capacity for loving greater than ours. He is Unique, Uncreated, Infinite, Totally Other than we are. He surpasses and transcends all human concepts, considerations and expectations. He is beyond anything we can intellectualize or imagine. That is why God is a *scandal* to men and women—because He cannot be comprehended by a finite mind.

Jesus calls us to stretch our minds and hearts, to renounce human standards of justice, mercy, love, rectitude and fair play. For a disciple of Jesus the process of spiritual growth is a gradual repudiation of the unreal image of God, an increasing openness to the true and living God. In my own life, honoring the First Commandment, "I am Yahweh your God: you shall have no gods except me," has meant repudiating the god of fear and wrath handed on to me by preachers, teachers and church authorities in my youth, repudiating the strange god who sees all non-Christians as good-for-nothings, who consigns all heathens to hell, who has given any one denomination a bonded franchise for salvation, who rubs his hands together with malicious glee and sends a Catholic to hell because he ate a hot dog on Friday, April 27, 1949. It has meant repudiating the strange god who flinches at gracing certain *other* churches with his presence; who despises a beleaguered couple who practice birth control; who forbids a divorcee the Eucharist; who ordains that some of his creatures (whether for race or creed or some other reason) shall be denied equal opportunity for employment and housing; who tells married Catholic priests that they are excommunicated and mature women that in America they can be vice president of the country but in the church they must sit down, submit and shut up.

This same spiritual process of repudiating unreal images of God can be found in the writings of the Hebrew prophets and in the work of spiritual formation that Jesus undertook with His first disciples. Because they had fashioned their own image of the Messiah, they resisted the mission of the real Messiah, asking Him impatiently when He would triumphantly reveal His power to Israel. They looked for an unreal messiah of their own making and found a real one of God's making—but only after they were dispossessed of all their illusions and expectations. Expectations are our subtle attempts to control God and manipulate mystery. We can get so wrapped up in them that when Jesus breaks into our lives in new and surprising ways, we neither recognize Him nor hear His message.

What was the message of Jesus concerning God? What did He really preach? What did He really reveal? Modern Scripture scholars tell us that if we want to be most confident that we are in touch with the original preaching of Jesus, we should turn to His parables—quick, decisive stories that make clear the fundamental points to His teaching. For our present purposes two will suffice:

First, in chapter 20 of Matthew, the parable of the crazy farmer. It was harvest time and the owner of the farm went repeatedly into the marketplace, the hiring hall of his day, to recruit workers for his fields. Given the time of year and the amount of work to be done, those who were still idling the day away with small talk at the eleventh hour must have been a lazy and shiftless bunch. Still, the farmer needed workers and even they were called into the field.

One presumes they took their time getting there, shuffled about and did a minimum of work. Then the surprise:

19

they were awarded a full day's pay! In this familiar parable as told by other rabbis of Jesus' day, those who arrived at the eleventh hour earned the whole day's pay because they worked extra hard. In Jesus' version, however, the emphasis is not on the diligence of the workers but on the gratuitous generosity of the farmer (presumably the families of the loafers depended on the income for their nightly meal). It was a mad, crazy, insanely generous act. No human farmer or businessman could behave that way and remain in business for very long. Even today, we are offended by this overpayment of loafers, freeloaders. The other workers certainly were. "The men who came last have put in only one hour," they complained, "and you've treated them the same as us, though we've done a heavy day's work in all the heat." And the farmer's answer: "My friends, I am not being unjust to you. Didn't we agree on your wage? Take your earnings and go. If I choose to pay the last-comer as much as you, haven't I the right to do what I like with my own?"

Two thousand years later the Christian community is still scandalized by divine generosity. In one of his plays, Jean Anouilh portrays the Last Judgment as he imagines it: The just are densely clustered at the gate of heaven eager to march in, sure of their reserved seats and bursting with impatience. Suddenly a rumor starts spreading. They look at one another in disbelief. "Look, He's going to forgive those others too." They gasp and sputter: "After all the trouble I went through. I just can't believe it." Exasperated, they work themselves into a fury and start cursing God. And at that very instant, they are damned. That was the final judgment, you see. They judged themselves, excommunicated themselves. Love appeared and they refused to acknowledge it. "We don't approve of a heaven that's open to every Tom, Dick and Harry. We spurn this God who lets everyone off. We can't love a God who loves so foolishly."

A parable in Luke 15 makes the same point. The prodigal son walks down the road rehearsing the penitent speech he will give. The father, rocking on the porch, sees him coming and dashes to meet him. The young man barely gets out the first sentence of his speech before the father embraces him, puts a new robe on him and proclaims a celebration. Hardly an appropriate way to deal with a delinquent son. The boy had been spoiled rotten in the first place; if the father spoils him again, how will he learn?

Haven't you identified with the other brother in this story muttering to himself: "Wonderful! All this while I've been sweating away, fattening the calf that my father is now going to roast for this dingbat. Dad's really off-the-wall!"

The French Easter liturgy says, *"L'amour de Dieu est folie"*—the love of God is foolishness. And Jesus says it is a foolishness that is meant to call forth joy. The farmer reproaches those who've worked the whole day because they are not willing to celebrate his generosity. The father is appalled when his older son will not join the joyful welcome-home party. "God's extravagant love," Jesus is saying, "demands a joyous response from us."

Both of these parables are a revelation from Jesus of the real God. But Jesus' image of God assaults our standards of justice and fair play. The very foundations of our religion are being shaken! The depraved good-for-nothing prodigal is preferred to his hard-working brother? Celebration instead of punishment! What kind of lunatic order is this that reverses all rank, making the last first and the first last? At the end all get the same reward?

The parables of Jesus reveal a God who is consistently overgenerous with His forgiveness and grace. He portrays God as the lender magnanimously canceling a debt, as the shepherd seeking a strayed sheep, as the judge

21

hearing the prayer of the tax collector. In Jesus' stories, divine forgiveness does not depend on our repentance or on our ability to love our enemies or on our doing heroic, virtuous deeds. God's forgiveness depends only on the love out of which He fashioned the human race.

The God of Judaism forgives the person who has changed his ways, done penance and shown that he is leading a better life. But under the old covenant there is no forgiveness for those who remain sinners: The sinner faces judgment. But the God of Jesus does not judge us, for He loves even those who are evil. In a word, the Father of Jesus loves sinners. He is the only God people have ever heard of who behaves this way. Unreal gods, the inventions of people, despise sinners. But the Father of Jesus loves all, no matter what they do. And this, of course, is almost too incredible for us to accept.

God does not condemn but forgives. The sinner is accepted even before he repents. Forgiveness is granted to him; he need only accept the gift. This is real amnesty—gratis. The Gospel of Jesus Christ is the love story of God with us. It begins with unconditional forgiveness: the sole condition is trusting faith. Christianity happens when men and women experience the unwavering trust and reckless confidence that come from knowing the God of Jesus. There is no reason for being wary, scrupulous, cautious or afraid with this God. As John writes in his first letter: "In love there can be no fear, but fear is driven out by perfect love: because to fear is to expect punishment, and anyone who is afraid is still imperfect in love" (1 John 4:18 JB).

God's love is based on nothing, and the fact that it is based on nothing makes us secure. Were it based on anything we do, and that "anything" were to collapse, then God's love would crumble as well. But with the God of Jesus no such thing can possibly happen. People who realize this can live freely and to the full. Remember Atlas, who carries the whole world? We have Christian Atlases who mistakenly carry the burden of trying to deserve God's love. Even the mere watching of this lifestyle is depressing. I'd like to say to Atlas: "Put that globe down and dance on it. That's why God made it." And to these weary Christian Atlases: "Lay down your load and build your life on God's love." We don't have to earn this love; neither do we have to support it. It is a free gift. Jesus calls out: "Come to Me, all you Atlases who are weary and find life burdensome, and I will refresh you."

When you visit a home for the mentally retarded, like Jean Vanier's *L'Arche,* the Ark, in Mobile, Alabama, you see people who have no worth in our productive society. They don't do anything. They are just there. Yet you never doubt that God loves them. The handicapped make us realize our handicaps. They strip off the masks we wear, the roles we play that give us a sense of earning our position with God and others. They challenge us to let go of everything we have taken literally, all our lives, to find our own symbols of the Holy One, to open ourselves to the mystery of the gracious God within us.

The unearned love of God can be disturbing. The idea of reward without work might put a brake on our dedication to the Gospel. I mean, why struggle to do good if God loves so recklessly and foolishly? It appears to be a sensible, valid question.

> But those who truly know the God of Jesus are not likely to ask why they should be laboring for the kingdom while others stand around all day idle. They want life and they have found the fullness of life in God Himself. . . . The rest of us may ask why we should bother to live uprightly if God is going to be so generous, but not those who have found the God of Jesus. Only when our inner vision is blocked by resentment, outrage, anger, or envy do we find ourselves threatened by God's love. The last prayer

of Jesus on the Cross, 'Father, forgive them. They know not what they do,' is a testament from one who knew what God is like.[1]

The love of God embodied in Jesus is radically different from our natural human way of loving. As a man, I am drawn to love appealing things and persons. I love the Jersey Shore and Clearwater Beach at sunset, Handel's *Messiah,* hot fudge sundaes and my family. There is a common denominator or, better, a common dynamic in all of them. I am attracted by certain qualities that I find congenial. When I love as a man, I am drawn by the good perceived in the other. I love someone for what I find in him or her.

> Now: unlike ourselves, the Father of Jesus loves men and women, not for what He finds in them, but for what lies within Himself. It is not because men and women are good that He loves them, nor only good men and women that He loves. It is because He is so unutterably good that He loves all persons, good and evil. . . . He loves the loveless, the unloving, the unlovable. He does not detect what is congenial, appealing, attractive, and respond to it with His favor. In fact, He does not respond at all. The Father of Jesus is a source. He acts; He does not react. He initiates love. He is love without motive.[2]

Jesus, who lives for those in whom love is dead, and died that His killers might live, reveals a Father who has no wrath. The Father cannot be offended, nor can He be pleased by what people do. This is the very opposite of indifference. The Lord does not cherish us as we deserve—if that were the case, we would be desolate—but as He must, unable to do otherwise. He is love. Hard as it is for us to believe—because we neither give nor receive love among ourselves in this way—we yet believe, because of the life-death-resurrection of the

Carpenter-Messiah, that His Father is more loving, more forgiving, more cherishing than Abraham, Isaac or Jacob could have dreamed.

What this says simply is that the God and Father of our Lord Jesus Christ is gracious. His love is gratuitous in a way that defies our imagination.

It is for this reason that we can proclaim with theological certainty in the power of the Word: *God loves you as you are and not as you should be!* Do you believe this? That God loves you beyond worthiness and unworthiness, beyond fidelity and infidelity, that He loves you in the morning sun and the evening rain, that He loves you without caution, regret, boundary, limit or breaking point?

I am *not* asking: Do you believe in love? That is abstract ideology. Agnostics and atheists can say that. What I am asking is: Can you say with conviction what the apostle John writes in his first letter: "I have come to know and believe in the love *God has for me*"? The last four words—"God has for me"—turn an abstract proposition into a personal relationship. This love is the content of our faith: It is a magnificent summary of all we believe. "The love God has for us" constitutes ultimate meaning and brings the peace and joy the world cannot give.

To believe means to realize not just with the head but also with the heart that God loves *me* in a creative, intimate, unique, reliable, and *tender* way. Creative: out of His love I came forth; through His love I am who I am. Intimate: His love reaches out to the deepest in me. Unique: His love embraces me as I am, not as I am considered to be by other people or supposed to be in my own self-image. Reliable: His love will never let me down. Tender . . .

Tenderness is what happens to you when you know you are deeply and sincerely *liked* by someone. If you communicate to me that you like me, not just love me

25

as a brother in Christ, you open up to me the possibility of self-respect, self-esteem and wholesome self-love. Your acceptance of me banishes my fears. My defense mechanisms—sarcasm, aloofness, name-dropping, self-righteousness, giving the appearance of having it all together—start to fall. I drop my mask and stop disguising my voice. You instill self-confidence in me and allow me to smile at my weaknesses and absurdities. The look in your eyes gives me permission to make the journey into the interior of myself and make peace with that part of myself with which I could never find peace before. I become more open, sincere, vulnerable and affectionate. I too grow tender.

Several years ago, Edward Farrell, a priest from Detroit, went on a two-week summer vacation to Ireland to visit relatives. His one living uncle was about to celebrate his eightieth birthday. On the great day, Ed and his uncle got up early. It was before dawn. They took a walk along the shores of Lake Killarney and stopped to watch the sunrise. They stood side by side for a full twenty minutes and then resumed walking. Ed glanced at his uncle and saw that his face had broken into a broad smile. Ed said, "Uncle Seamus, you look very happy." "I am." Ed asked, "How come?" And his uncle replied, "The Father of Jesus is very fond of me."

If the question were put to you, "Do you honestly believe that God *likes* you?"—not loves you, because theologically He must—how would you answer? God loves by necessity of His nature; without the eternal, interior generation of love, He would cease to be God. But if you could answer, "The Father is very fond of me," there would come a relaxedness, a serenity and a compassionate attitude toward yourself that is a reflection of God's own tenderness. In Isaiah 49:15, God says: "Does a woman forget her baby at the breast, or fail to cherish the son of her womb? Yet even if these forget, I will never forget you" (JB).

One spiritual writer has observed that human beings are born with two diseases: life, from which we die; and hope, which says the first disease is not terminal. Hope is built into the structure of our personalities, into the depths of our unconscious; it plagues us to the very moment of our death. The critical question is whether hope is self-deception, the ultimate cruelty of a cruel and tricky universe, or whether it is just possibly the imprint of reality.

The parables of Jesus responded to that question. In effect Jesus said: Hope your wildest hopes, dream your maddest dreams, imagine your most fantastic fantasies. Where your hopes and your dreams and your imagination leave off, the love of My heavenly Father only begins. For "eye hath not seen, nor ear heard, neither have entered into the heart of man, the things which God hath prepared for them that love him" (1 Corinthians 2:9 KJV).

Shortly after I was ordained, I took a graduate course at Duquesne University in Pittsburgh. The professor was an old Dutchman who told the following story:

"I'm one of thirteen children. One day when I was playing in the street of our hometown in Holland, I got thirsty and came into the pantry of our house for a glass of water. It was around noon and my father had just come home from work to have lunch. He was sitting at the kitchen table having a glass of beer with a neighbor. A door separated the kitchen from the pantry and my father didn't know I was there. The neighbor said to my father, 'Joe, there's something I've wanted to ask you for a long time, but if it's too personal, just forget I ever asked.'

" 'What is your question?'

" 'Well, you have thirteen children. Out of all of them, is there one that is your favorite, one you love more than all the others?' "

The professor continued his story: "I had my ear pressed against the door hoping against hope it would be me. 'That's easy,' my father said. 'Sure there's one I love more than all the others. That's Mary, the twelve-year-old. She just got braces on her teeth and feels so awkward and embarrassed that she won't go out of the house anymore. Oh, but you asked about my favorite. That's my twenty-three-year-old, Peter. His fiancée just broke their engagement, and he is desolate. But the one I really love the most is little Michael. He's totally uncoordinated and terrible in any sport he tries to play. The other kids on the street make fun of him. But, of course, the apple of my eye is Susan. Only twenty-four, living in her own apartment and developing a drinking problem. I cry for Susan. But I guess of all the kids . . .' and my father went on mentioning each of his thirteen children by name."

The professor ended his story, saying: "What I learned was that the one my father loved most was the one who needed him most at that time. And that's the way the Father of Jesus is: He loves those most who need Him most, who rely on Him, depend upon Him and trust Him in everything. Little He cares whether you've been as pure as St. John or as sinful as the prostitute in Simon the Pharisee's house. All that matters is trust. It seems to me that learning how to trust God defines the meaning of Christian living. God doesn't wait until we have our moral life in order before He starts loving us."

Again, though, that nagging question: Won't the awareness that God loves us no matter what lead to spiritual laziness and moral laxity? Theoretically, this seems a reasonable fear, but in reality the opposite is true. You know that your wife loves you as you are and not as you should be. Is this an invitation to infidelity, indifference, an "anything goes" attitude? On the contrary. Love calls forth love. Doing your own thing in complete freedom means, in fact, responding to her love. The more rooted we are in the love of God the more generously we live our faith and practice it.

It is this love that enables us to love ourselves without excuses and without questioning. We love ourselves as we are because faith has convinced us that God does so. We no longer worry about our spiritual growth (which is just another form of idolatry anyway). In living out being-loved, we move beyond the oppressive demands we impose on ourselves, beyond the idealistic claims of the ego that tells me who I should be, must be, ought to be. My friend Sister Mary Michael O'Shaughnessy has a banner in her room that says, "Today I will not *should* on myself." I don't have to be somebody else—Mother Teresa, Saint Francis, or Billy Graham. As my spiritual director Larry Hein says: "Be who you is, because if you is who you ain't, you ain't who you is."

It is always true to some extent that we make our images of God. It is even truer that our image of God makes us. Eventually we become like the God we image. One of the most beautiful fruits of knowing the God of Jesus is a compassionate attitude toward ourselves. Faith in the God of Jesus nurtures free, confident people. The God of love fosters a loving people. Jesus' experiences of God made Him the person He was. It freed Him from all self-concern and enabled Him to relate to people with warmth, ease, sympathy and liberating love.

This is why Scripture attaches such importance to *knowing* God. Healing our image of God heals our image of ourselves. Yahweh laments through the prophet Hosea, "My people know me not. It is love I desire, not sacrifices; *knowledge of God,* not holocausts" (see Hosea 6).

And John declares, "Eternal life is this: to know you, the only true God, and Jesus Christ whom you have sent" (John 17:3 JB). God's love becomes flesh and blood in the person of Jesus. In Him it receives hands and feet, a face and a voice. The purpose of the incarnation was

29

to convince us of the faithful love of God: "The reason I was born, the reason why I came into the world, is to testify to the truth." Truth in the Bible is the reliability of God's love. John in his prologue gives us the key to the life of Jesus: "We saw his glory, the glory that is his as the only Son of the Father, full of grace and truth" (John 1:14 JB).

Paul, who understood the mind and heart of Jesus better than any man or woman who has ever lived, prays in Ephesians 3:16–19: "I pray . . . that Christ may live in your hearts through faith, and then, planted in love and built on love, you will with all the saints have strength to grasp the breadth and the length, the height and depth; until, knowing the love of Christ, which is beyond all knowledge, you are filled with the utter fullness of God" (JB).

My brothers and sisters, this is the message. Some might quibble about the details, but there would not be, I think, much debate among contemporary Scripture scholars that this is the essence of the Good News of Jesus Christ. In healing our image of God, Jesus frees us of fear of the Father and dislike of ourselves.

> The old religious image of a vindictive, mean, and jealous God gives way in Jesus to the God of faith who cherishes people, all people, and has made his abode with them. Jesus presented a God who does not demand but gives; does not oppress but raises up; does not wound but heals. A God who forgives instead of condemning, and liberates instead of punishing. Woe then to those who demand, oppress, wound, and condemn, and punish in His name. It can only be said that they do not truly know him.[3]

Do we know Him? Do we know the God of Jesus Christ? Maybe we think that there are other things more important in the Christian walk than knowing God—like loving God, praising Him, thanking Him, keeping the commandments, living a good life. There are many things that make up a truly Christian life, but all of them are rooted in authentic knowledge of God.

Perhaps we think that because we are Christians and read the Bible and know a great deal *about* God, therefore we know God. Nothing could be further from the truth. It does us little good to memorize chapter and verse, to master the language of the Bible, if we have nothing to share in that language, no *experiential knowledge* of God in our lives.

Maybe that doesn't happen because we pray so little, so infrequently and so poorly. For everything else we have plenty of leisure time. Visits, get-togethers, movies, the Olympics, concerts, an evening with friends, an invitation we can't decline—and these things are good because it is right and natural to come together with friends. But most of our lives we are, as Søren Kierkegaard notes, "so busy" with other things that we don't have time to wait patiently to hear the voice of the God of Jesus within us. An appointment with the barber or hairdresser is inviolable, but when God lays claim to our time, we balk.

The most important thing that ever happens in prayer is letting ourselves be loved by God. "Be still, and know that I am God" (Psalm 46:10). It's like slipping into a tub of hot water and letting God's love wash over us, enfold us. Prayer is like sunbathing. When you spend a lot of time in the sun, people notice it. They say, "You've been at the beach." You look like you've been out in the sun because you've got a tan. Prayer—or bathing in the Son of God's love (Son bathing?)—makes you look different. The awareness of being loved brings a touch of lightness and a tint of brightness, and sometimes, for no apparent reason, a smile plays at the corner of your mouth. Through prayer you not only know God's love, you realize it; you are in conscious communion with it.

31

FOR REFLECTION

Begin with five minutes of silent prayer, becoming aware in faith of God's indwelling presence and humbly asking the Spirit to speak to your heart through Scripture, personal reflection and the insights of others.

Let one of the group read aloud 1 John 4:16–19. Then focus on the following questions for personal reflection and group interaction.

1. Describe the God you believed in during your childhood and teenage years.
2. Has anything changed in your perception of God, or are you still limping along with the understanding of God provided by your parents, pastors and your local faith community?
3. At this stage of the journey, are you too busy to spend time with God? Parents with small children surely qualify here. Have you lost the desire for holy loitering? Describe your prayer life.

CHAPTER 2

The Day I Met Jesus

t all began with a dream. In 1955 I was a sophomore at the University of Missouri, enrolled in the school of journalism. Early that October word came that I had won first prize of $100 in a short story contest sponsored by the university magazine, *Show Me*. It was a real feather in my cap as Missouri boasts one of the four best journalism schools in the country. One hundred dollars was big bucks in those days. Coupling it with the $110 monthly check I received from the GI Bill, I was financially secure. Further, I was informed that the prestigious fiction magazine *The New Yorker* would be looking at my future literary efforts with the promise of a job after graduation. *The New Yorker* is like Tiffany for the *trés chic,* ultrasophisticated set. I was engaged to a beautiful girl named Barbara, and we planned to marry the following year.

33

Other twenty-one-year-olds might be confused and uncertain about the direction of their lives, but not me. I was a seasoned veteran of the Marine Corps. Career and romance were humming smoothly. I was playing with a full deck, knew where I was going and was rowing rhythmically with both oars in the water. I felt I was a cut above my classmates, shaped in a different mold. There was only a faint resemblance between me and my unenlightened, immature peers who were still shifting the heavy suitcase from one hand to the other.

Then came the dream that blew my boat out of the water. In the dream I was driving a Cadillac up a steep hill, and the scene seemed more real than reality. At the crest of the hill was a fourteen-room ranch-style house with a panoramic view of the valley below. My name was on the mailbox. Parked in the driveway were a Lincoln and a Porsche. Inside the house Barbara was baking bread and the voices of four kids ranging from eight to eighteen rang out to greet me. I looked in the rearview mirror and decided my white hair needed a trim: I seemed to be between forty-five and fifty years old. As I opened the front door of our house, I noticed the plaque hanging prominently on the wall. It was the Nobel prize for literature awarded to me.

I awakened from the dream in a cold sweat, shouting, "O God, there's got to be more!" Am I going to invest the next twenty-five years of my life struggling to achieve fame, success, wealth and happy domesticity—and discover that that is all there is? A tremendous restlessness overcame me and a deep dissatisfaction. Why couldn't I be content with the ordinary joys of a normal person? How could this "something more" be so pressing and urgent if I didn't even know what it was? But there was no turning back. Unsettled and bewildered, I embarked on the search for God.

Breaking my engagement to Barbara was a carefully orchestrated disaster. Away at school, I hadn't seen her for four months, though I called her every Saturday night and wrote her rambling love letters, some as long as fifty-five pages, immortal prose that I imagined one day would be enshrined in the library of great books.

My plan to break the news to Barbara that I had gotten religion, had no more time for romance and was off to the seminary was, I thought, simple and ingenious. The night I arrived back in Brooklyn I called her from my parents' house and told her I would be at her house in an hour and to please have her parents present as I had a major announcement to make. (It never crossed my mind that she thought I wanted to move our wedding up and get married over Christmas.) I put on my charcoal black suit and borrowed a black tie from my father, hoping that Barbara would get the hint of my clerical calling.

Nervous and apprehensive, I planned on ringing her doorbell, then ushering her and her parents into the parlor to make the solemn proclamation. Her mother and father would be dumbstruck with awe and reverence; Barbara would weep briefly and then give me joyfully to God. I just hoped no one would try to kiss my hand. I would withdraw humbly and pompously at the same time, and a new chapter in my life would begin.

The real scenario was quite different. Barbara's parents had conveniently gone out so we could be alone. Even the door was left ajar so I didn't get the chance to do my ring-the-bell trick. Barbara was lying on the sofa, her fingers playing with her long black hair. She never looked so voluptuous. Four long months of absence suddenly staked their imperious claim. I dove onto the sofa, and we played kissy-face and huggy-bear for over an hour. Then we finally sat up at opposite ends of the sofa, and I lit a cigarette, glanced at her (I still blush when I think about this) and said, "Oh, by the way . . ."

She laughed so hard (she had an infectious kind of laugh) that soon I was roaring too. When I finally persuaded her that I was serious, she was furious, telling me that I had deceived her, was playing both ends against the middle, had selfishly just wanted a girlfriend until the seminary thing. I understood where she was coming from because I couldn't believe it myself. We reached an impasse. I stumbled out the door hurt, confused and wondering if I needed professional help. It was a painful memory, assuaged years later when I learned that Barbara was very happily married with a flock of children.

When I announced to my own family at Christmas that I planned to enter the Franciscan seminary in Loretto, Pennsylvania, in February, they were agitated and confused. I had not been a religious person. I went to Mass on Sunday and scrupulously observed the Sixth Commandment—true grit. But God was an unknown entity—remote and kind of frightening. I liked Walter Cronkite better. Not once in my life had I ever uttered the name of Jesus, and when I heard someone else use it, I bowed my head. I even bowed my head when somebody said *exegesis*. You can't be too careful when you know the great hangman in the sky hovers overhead.

My brother Rob was incredulous. He downed his pint of Schaefer beer and said, "I'll betcha fifty bucks you don't last a week in the seminary." We shook hands and both reached for another Schaefer.

The seminary exceeded my worst expectations. February in the Allegheny Mountains is razor-sharp cold exacerbated by bone-chilling winds. Upon my arrival, I was greeted as "Brother Richard." I hated that. Only Protestants called people "Brother," and I'd been brought up to be very suspicious of Protestants. My eighth-grade religion teacher told me that only Roman Catholics were in the bark of Peter and everyone else was drowning and going to hell. The third day at the seminary marked my investiture in the Franciscan Order, and I was robed with an ankle-length cassock and a white cord around my waist to tuck in the fluff. My first trip up a flight of stairs was humiliating. A macho marine walking up the inside of his cassock. I felt like a helpless, fickle, flaky female—and females, I was told, were now to be treated like the enemy.

Morning reveille sounded at 5:00 A.M. with some enthusiast screaming, "Benidicamus Domino." Nobody had told me about the Great Silence, which was to be observed until breakfast around eight o'clock. The brothers were to answer dutifully, "Deo Gratias," and move about in strictest silence. I glanced at the window and shouted, "Good God, it's pitch black. Why are we up at this hour?" Father Augustine stood in the doorway and wrote my name in a black book.

In chapel we opened our prayer books to chant psalms in Latin. Latin, for heaven's sake. With the Korean War just ended and my sergeant's stripes tattooed on my brain, I'm singing in Latin? I looked at the other clerics. They appeared enraptured. I couldn't even pronounce the words. *Fakers* was my verdict on that psalm-singing crowd of pantywaists.

That night at dinner Father Augustine passed me the bowl of peas. "Thank you, but I don't like peas." Under holy obedience he made me eat the whole bowl. One thing for sure about the seminary—I was learning how to hate.

Each brother was assigned a household task. Mine was to dust the parlor—to me the most demeaning of all domestic chores. I was piddling around dusting under the doilies when my eye caught an eight-day Swiss clock atop the mantel, covered with a large glass bowl. I was staring at it when Father Augustine walked in. "What are you doing, Brother Richard?" Again I shuddered internally at his oblique Protestantism and wondered if he were a Commie.

"I was wondering how much beer that glass bowl would hold." He made another entry in his black book.

After seven days, I decided to pack it in. They were going to kick me out anyway. I'd lasted the week, so I could collect the fifty bucks from my brother. I hoped Barbara would still be drying her tears. I would commend her for her patience and undying love, we would be reconciled, I would return to Missouri and we would be married in June. A narrow escape from my flirtation with death.

I packed my suitcase and went to Father Augustine's office to inform him of my departure. He wasn't there. I decided to stop at the chapel and say goodbye to God. "Thank You, God (this is Richie), for showing me that the priesthood is not my calling. Please have Barbara waiting when I get back to Brooklyn. As a sign of my goodwill, I'll go to Mass one extra time a week for a whole year. [I thought that would impress Him that He wasn't dealing with some shallow soul.] Well, goodbye, God. I'll catch You in Brooklyn."

I returned to the seat of power, but Augustine still had not arrived. Never one to shun the heroic, I decided to go back to the chapel and do something great for God. Even though it wasn't required, I would visit each of the fourteen "stations of the cross." I grabbed a book and followed the directions. At the first station, "Jesus is condemned to death," I read the prayer, made a hasty genuflection like I'd smelled smoke in the building, and hurried on to the second one. *Maybe when I'm working for* The New Yorker, I thought, *I'll rewrite these archaic prayers, put them in modern idiom and do the church a favor. Maybe the pope will make me a Knight of St. Gregory or something.*

After eleven minutes of praying and genuflecting, I checked into the twelfth station, "Jesus died on the Cross." The rubric in the book said "kneel." As I sank to my knees, the Angelus bell from the cloistered Carmelite monastery three miles away sounded in the distance. It was noon. At five minutes after *three,* I rose from my knees and went in search of a Bible. I had never read the Bible before but knew that I had to read the Gospels. I couldn't find one in the monastery. In those days, it was considered a Protestant book.

During those three hours on my knees, I felt like a little boy kneeling at the seashore. Little waves washed up and lapped at my knees. Slowly the waves grew bigger and stronger till they reached my waist. Suddenly a tremendous wave of concussion force knocked me over backward and swept me off the beach, reeling in midair, arching through space, vaguely aware that I was being carried to a place I had never been before—the heart of Jesus Christ. When He called my name, it was not Richie or Brennan, but another word that I shall not disclose, a word that is my very own name, spoken with infinite love. It is the sweetest sound I shall ever hear, the name by which Jesus knows me. It must be what Mary Magdalene responded to when Jesus in the garden said simply, "Mary"—except that in my case He did not call me by my given name.

In this first-ever-in-my-life experience of being unconditionally loved, I moved back and forth between mild ecstasy and hushed trembling. The aura was what George Maloney years later would describe as "bright darkness." And bewildering strength. The moment lingered on and on in a timeless *now* until without warning I felt a hand grip my heart. I could barely breathe. It was abrupt and startling. The awareness of being loved was no longer gentle, tender and comfortable. The love of Christ, the crucified Son of God, for me, took on the wildness, passion and fury of a sudden spring storm. Like a bursting dam, spasms of convulsive crying erupted from the depths of my being. He died on the cross for me! I had known that before, but in the ways that Cardinal Newman describes as notional knowledge—abstract, far away, largely irrelevant to the gut issues of life, just another trinket in the dusty pawnshop of dogmatic beliefs.

But in the one blinding moment of salvific truth, it was *real* knowledge calling for personal engagement of my mind and heart. Christianity was no longer simply a moral code but a love affair, the thrill, the excitement, the incredible, passionate joy of being loved and falling in love with Jesus Christ.

At last, drained, spent, feeling limp and lost in speechless humility, I was back kneeling at the seashore with quiet, calm waves of love sweeping over me like a gentle tide, saturating my mind and heart in a tranquil mode of deepest worship.

When at 3:05 P.M. I rose shakily from the floor, glanced at my watch in disbelief, resonated with awe and wonder and, unable to find a Bible, returned to my cell and unpacked my bag, I knew that the most thrilling adventure of my life had just begun. It was a new mode of existence, and Paul describes it well in Colossians 3:11: "There is only Christ: he is everything" (JB).

Thirty years later I would like to share with you a few selections set down over many years in a little red and green plaid blank book. I call it "The Journal of the Journey." The following I copied there from the writings of a Trappist monk:

> Our response to Jesus Christ will be total the day we experience how total is his love for us. Instead of our self-conscious efforts to be good, we should allow ourselves the luxury of letting ourselves be loved by God. And much of his love for us will be expressed through the medium of our friends' love for us. How else could he reveal it in a way that is tangible? "You are my friends if you do what I command. . . . This is my command: Love each other" (John 15:14, 17).

Imagine right this moment that Jesus walks in the door, comes up to you, looks you squarely in the eye and calls you by one word. What is that word? What is the word that God knows you by, that is the entire sum of God's knowledge of you and relationship to you? It will define your whole being. Is it a condemnatory word, a judging word, a congratulatory word, a word of affection? "To those who prove victorious I will give . . . a white stone—a stone with a new name written on it, known only to the man who receives it" (Revelation 2:17 JB).

Now imagine that the human person who loves you and knows more about you than anyone else in the world does the same thing. This person is known to you by the constancy of his or her relationship to you. Through thick or thin, he or she has stuck by you, though this faithfulness has often been tested. When that person says the word by which he or she knows you, what is it? Is it the same word by which Jesus knows you?

> I do not think we are truly ourselves or truly whole until we have heard that word from another human being. For most of us, deaf and full of preconceptions about ourselves, the word must be spoken repeatedly before we finally hear it. It penetrates only when we are absolutely convinced that it is being said by someone who knows us thoroughly. . . . It even makes God happy because another person has heard and accepted the [love He has for us]. . . . That word is the sweetest sound we will ever hear.
>
> In exchange, God has given us His own Name so that we will know Him also. Jesus has revealed the name of God to be *Abba,* a daddy whose fatherhood extends to all who believe in His Son.[1]

FOR REFLECTION

Begin with five minutes of silent prayer, becoming aware in faith of God's indwelling presence and humbly asking the Spirit to speak to your heart through Scripture, personal reflection and the insights of others.

Let one of the group read aloud Philippians 3:7–11. Then focus on the following questions for personal reflection and group interaction.

1. One hundred years ago in the Deep South, the phrase "born again" was seldom used. Rather, the words used to describe the breakthrough into a personal relationship with Jesus were, "I was seized by the power of a great affection." It was a deeply human and moving way to describe the initiative of God, the explosion within the human heart when Jesus became Lord of one's personal and professional life. It lent new meaning to the old Russian proverb, "Those who have the disease called Jesus will never be cured." Share your own experience of the breakthrough.

2. If it has not happened as yet, do you remain confident that it will come to pass?

3. What has developed in your spiritual life since you were seized by the power of a great affection? Are you still clinging to that moment?

CHAPTER 3

Freedom under the Word

There are two visions of life, two kinds of people. The first see life as a possession to be carefully guarded. They are called *settlers*. The second see life as a wild, fantastic, explosive gift. They are called *pioneers*.

These two types give rise to two kinds of theology: Settler Theology and Pioneer Theology. According to Wes Seeliger in his book *Western Theology,* the first kind, Settler Theology, is an attempt to answer all the questions, define and housebreak some sort of Supreme Being, establish the status quo on golden tablets in cinemascope. Pioneer Theology is an attempt to talk about what it means to receive the strange gift of life. The Wild West is the setting for both theologies.

In Settler Theology the *church* is the courthouse. It is the center of town life. The old stone structure dominates the town square. Its windows are small, and this makes things dark inside. Within the courthouse walls, records are kept, taxes collected, trials held for bad guys. The courthouse is the settler's symbol of law, order, stability and—most important—security. The mayor's office is on the top floor. His eagle eye ferrets out the smallest details of town life.

In Pioneer Theology the *church* is the covered wagon. It's a house on wheels, always on the move. The covered wagon is where the pioneers eat, sleep, fight, love and die. It bears the marks of life and movement—it creaks, is scarred with arrows, bandaged with bailing wire. The covered wagon is always where the action is. It moves toward the future and doesn't bother to glorify its own ruts. The old wagon isn't comfortable, but the pioneers don't mind. They are more into adventure than comfort.

In Settler Theology *God* is the mayor. He is a sight to behold. Dressed like a dude from back East, he lounges in an overstuffed chair in his courthouse office. He keeps the blinds drawn. No one sees him or knows him directly, but since there is order in the town, who can deny that he is there? The mayor is predictable and always on schedule. The settlers fear the mayor but look to him to clear the payroll and keep things going. Peace and quiet are the mayor's main concerns. That's why he sends the sheriff to check on pioneers who ride into town.

In Pioneer Theology *God* is the trail boss. He is rough and rugged, full of life. He chews tobacco, drinks straight whiskey. The trail boss lives, eats, sleeps, fights with his people. Their well-being is his concern. Without him the wagon wouldn't move; living as a freeman would be impossible. The trail boss often gets down in the mud with the pioneers to help push the wagon, which often gets stuck. He prods the pioneers when they get soft and want to turn back. His fist is an expression of his concern.

44

In Settler Theology *Jesus* is the sheriff. He's the guy who is sent by the mayor to enforce the rules. He wears a white hat, drinks milk, outdraws the bad guys. The sheriff decides who is thrown into jail. There is a saying in town that goes: "Those who believe that the mayor sent the sheriff, and follow the rules—they won't stay in Boothill when it comes their time."

In Pioneer Theology *Jesus* is the scout. He rides out ahead to find out which way the pioneers should go. He lives all the dangers of the trail. The scout suffers every hardship, is attacked by the Indians. Through his words and actions he reveals the true intentions of the trail boss. By looking at the scout, those on the trail learn what it means to be a pioneer.

In Settler Theology the *Holy Spirit* is the saloon girl. Her job is to comfort the settlers. They come to her when they feel lonely or when life gets dull or dangerous. She tickles them under the chin and makes everything okay again. The saloon girl squeals to the sheriff when someone starts disturbing the peace.

In Pioneer Theology the *Holy Spirit* is the buffalo hunter. He rides along with the covered wagon and furnishes fresh meat for the pioneers. Without it they would die. The buffalo hunter is a strange character— sort of a wild man. The pioneers never can tell what he will do next. He scares the hell out of the settlers. He has a big black gun that goes off like a cannon. He rides into town on Sunday to shake up the settlers. You see, every Sunday morning, the settlers have a little ice cream party in the courthouse. With his gun in hand the buffalo hunter sneaks up to one of the courthouse windows. He fires a tremendous blast that rattles the whole courthouse. Men jump out of their skin, women scream, dogs bark. Chuckling to himself, the buffalo hunter rides back to the wagon train shooting up the town as he goes.

In Settler Theology the *Christian* is the settler. He fears the open unknown frontier. His concern is to stay on good terms with the mayor and keep out of the sheriff's way. "Safety first" is his motto. To him the courthouse is a symbol of security, peace, order and happiness. He keeps his money in the bank. The banker is his best friend. The settler never misses an ice cream party.

In Pioneer Theology the *Christian* is the pioneer. He is a man of daring, hungry for new life. He rides hard, knows how to use a gun when necessary. The pioneer feels sorry for the settlers and tries to tell them of the joy and fulfillment of life on the trail. He dies with his boots on.

In Settler Theology the *clergyman* is the banker. Within his vault are locked the values of the town. He is a highly respected man. He has a gun but keeps it hidden in his desk. He feels that he and the sheriff have a lot in common. After all, they both protect the bank.

In Pioneer Theology the *clergyman* is the cook. He doesn't furnish the meat. He just dishes up what the buffalo hunter provides. This is how he supports the movement of the wagon. He never confuses his job with that of the trail boss, scout or buffalo hunter. He sees himself as just another pioneer who has learned to cook. The cook's job is to help the pioneers pioneer.

In Settler Theology *faith* is trusting in the safety of the town: obeying the laws, keeping your nose clean, believing the mayor is in the courthouse.

In Pioneer Theology *faith* is the spirit of adventure. The readiness to move out. To risk everything on the trail. Faith is obedience to the restless voice of the trail boss.

In Settler Theology *sin* is breaking one of the town's ordinances.

In Pioneer Theology *sin* is wanting to turn back.

In Settler Theology *salvation* is living close to home and hanging around the courthouse.

46

In Pioneer Theology *salvation* is being more afraid of sterile town life than of death on the trail. Salvation is joy at the thought of another day to push on into the unknown. It is trusting the trail boss and following his scout while living on the meat provided by the buffalo hunter.

The settlers and the pioneers portray in cowboy-movie language the people of the law and the people of the Spirit. In the time of the historical Jesus, the guardians of the ecclesiastical setup, the scribes and Pharisees and Sadducees, had ensconced themselves in the courthouse and enslaved themselves to the law. This not only enhanced their prestige in society, it also gave them a sense of security. People fear the responsibility of being free. It is often easier to let others make the decisions or to rely upon the letter of the law. Some people *want* to be slaves.

After enslaving themselves to the letter of the law, such people always go on to deny freedom to others. They will not rest until they have imposed the same oppressive burdens upon others. Jesus described them this way: "They tie up heavy loads and put them on men's shoulders, but they themselves are not willing to lift a finger to move them" (Matthew 23:4).

Jesus wanted to liberate His people from the law— from all laws. Under His Word we become free, people of the Spirit, and the fellowship of free people grows up, as in the New Testament, beyond all kinds of theological disagreement.

Paul writes in Galatians 5:1, "It is for freedom that Christ has set us free. Stand firm, then, and do not let yourselves be burdened again by a yoke of slavery." If we are not experiencing what Paul calls in Romans 8:21 "the glorious freedom of the children of God," then we must acknowledge that His Word has not taken sovereign possession of us, that we are not fully under the sway of His Spirit.

I once asked a group of graduating seniors from a Catholic college, "At this point, what does it mean to you to be a Christian?" Their answers were so similar in content that I reduced them to a single paragraph that read: "To be a Christian means that I must go to Mass on Sunday; I can't eat meat on Ash Wednesday and Good Friday; I can't practice birth control, get a divorce, procure an abortion or see an X-rated movie."

For many people in the church, Christianity is not Good News. The Gospel is not the glad tidings of freedom and salvation proclaimed by Christ Jesus but a rigid code of dos and don'ts, a tedious moralizing, a list of minimum requirements for avoiding the pains of hell.

In the Gospel of John the one theme and the only theme with multiple variations is: Do we know Jesus? To know Him is life. Everything else fades into twilight and darkness. The German Scripture scholar Ernst Kasemann remarks:

> What causes most trouble for Christians of all ages is not legalism or lack of faith or theological controversies; it is Jesus Himself, who bestows freedom so openhandedly and dangerously on those who do not know what to do with it. The church always gets panic-stricken for fear of the turmoil that Christ creates when He comes on the scene; and so it takes His freedom under its own management for the protection of the souls entrusted to it, in order to dispense it in homeopathic doses when it seems necessary. The church claims to represent Jesus on earth, but in fact it often supplants Him. It must tremble in all its joints when confronted with His portrait. Ecclesiastical traditions and laws have domesticated Jesus, and today all the churches are living off the success of the attempt.

Kasemann's words are a prophetic cry to return to our origins; to remember who is the Founder of the Firm; to ask, "Is Jesus the criterion of the church or is the church the criterion of Jesus?" (In this context, I offer one observation on the theological controversy swirling around open Communion and the requisite conditions for receiving the bread and the cup. Anyone who is allowed to hear the preaching of the Word on Sunday morning should be permitted to partake of the Lord's Supper. For Christ comes to the ungodly, and His coming ends ungodliness and makes us worthy, provided we do not refuse to accept Him. To fail to honor the initiative of Jesus in seeking out the lost leads to an utterly ungodly and unchristian preoccupation with works that would make us worthy!)

Suppose it were so ordained that your whole future, your eternal destiny, was to depend on your personal relationship with the bishop of your area. Wouldn't you arrange to spend considerably more time with him than you do now? Wouldn't you try with his help to overcome all the character defects and personality traits that you knew were displeasing to him? And suppose business obligations called you away to that city of saints and scholars, Brooklyn, New York. Wouldn't you drop him frequent notes from there and be eager to return to him "as the deer pants for streams of water" (Psalm 42:1)?

And if he confided to you that he kept a diary of personal memoirs, which were the deepest whisperings of his inner self, wouldn't you be eager not only to read them but to steep yourself in them so that you might know and love him more?

These are burning questions that every disciple must answer in total candor. Do you hunger for Jesus Christ? Do you yearn to spend time alone with Him in prayer? Is He the most important person in your life? Does He fill your soul like a song of joy? Is He on your lips as a shout of praise? Do you eagerly turn to His memoirs, His personal testament, His Gospels, to learn more of Him? Are you making the effort to die to anything and everything that would inhibit, diminish or threaten your friendship?

To discern where you *really* are with the Lord, recall what has saddened you recently. Was it the realization that you don't love Jesus enough? That you do not seek His face in prayer often enough? That you can't honestly say that the greatest thing that ever happened in your life is that Jesus came to you and you heard His voice? That you do not regard finding Jesus as your supreme happiness? That you have denied His last commandment by not loving His people enough?

Or have you been saddened and depressed over a lack of human respect, criticism from an authority figure, financial problems, lack of friends, your bulging waistline?

On the other hand, what has *gladdened* you recently? Reflecting on your election to the Christian community? The joy of praying, "Abba, I belong to you"? The afternoon you stole away with the Gospel as your only companion? The thrilling awareness that God loves you unconditionally just as you are and not as you should be? A small victory over selfishness? Or were the sources of your gladness and joy a new car, a Brooks Brothers suit, a movie and a pizza, a trip to Paris or Peoria? Are you worshiping idols?

When our lives are governed not by a network of laws but by the fire of the Spirit that burns within, when we submit to the saving truth that we reach life only through death, that we come to light only through darkness, that the grain of wheat must fall into the ground and die, that Jonah must be buried in the belly of the whale, that the alabaster jar of self must be broken if others are to perceive the sweet fragrance of Christ, when we respond to the call of Jesus, which is not, "Come to the ice cream party," but, *"Come to Me,"* then the limitless power of the Holy Spirit will be unleashed with astonishing force.

It is more than mere coincidence that the prophet and teacher who wrote the letter to the Hebrews should describe Jesus in chapter 2, verse 10, as "the pioneer of [our] salvation" (RSV). Again in chapter 12, verse 2, of the same letter, Jesus is "the pioneer and perfecter of our faith" (RSV). By looking at Jesus we learn what it is to be on the trail to abundant life.

Jesus liberated His disciples from the tyranny of law. He did this not by abolishing or changing the law but by dethroning it from its place of primacy, relativizing it, making it subordinate to love and compassion—to the law of the Spirit.

In Romans 7:1–6, Paul affirms that in Christ we are no longer under the law's domination. Just as a wife through the death of her husband is no longer bound to the law of matrimony, so the Christian living in the Spirit released by the risen Jesus is no longer bound to the outward letter. In Galatians 3 Paul vehemently makes war on the position that said if a man observes the law, he is saved. *No,* says Paul. The Christian, united to the risen Christ, is dead to the law, delivered from the law, freed once and for all. The Christian vocation is a vocation to liberty. Freedom is the cornerstone of Christianity.

What then? Is the Christian free to do his own thing, to sin with abandon? Again Paul answers *no:* "Do not use your freedom to indulge the sinful nature" (Galatians 5:13).

What then is the norm or standard by which a Christian can guide his actions and shape his moral behavior? Paul replies, "The law of the Spirit of life set me free from the law of sin and death" (Romans 8:2).

What is the law of the Spirit? Paul sees it as a vital, dynamic internal force. More precisely the law of the Spirit is the Holy Spirit, the love between the Father and Son. Jesus said, "If anyone loves me, he will obey my

51

teaching. My Father will love him, and we will come to him and make our home with him" (John 14:23). Jesus spoke of the life of grace in terms of indwelling our hearts by His own Spirit. And the Spirit impels us, as He impelled Jesus, to live as a child of God. The new law is the Spirit within us giving us life in Christ Jesus. And so Paul opens chapter 8 of Romans with the triumphant cry: "There is now no condemnation for those who are in Christ Jesus. . . . The law of the Spirit of life set me free from the law of sin and death" (vv. 1–2).

But freedom ends when Jesus Himself is lost to view, when He cannot get a hearing through the ecclesiastical setup, when He is ignored in favor of legalizing, moralizing, philosophizing, and so we erect new temples to an unknown god.

Nevertheless, the Word of God stands: "If the Son sets you free, you will be free indeed" (John 8:36). Again Paul insists our liberty is not a license for lust. "You, my brothers, were called to be free. But do not use your freedom to indulge the sinful nature" (Galatians 5:13). Here Paul echoes the teaching of Jesus that the good tree will bear good fruit. Christian action follows Christian being. We must live out in our lives what we are. Christian existence means that we have been transformed. Through the Spirit we live in Christ Jesus. Life is doing what comes supernaturally. *Noblesse oblige.* Nobility obliges. The child of a king must not live like a peasant.

Thus for the Christian, there is no law but the Spirit. There is no need for law; a child doesn't have to be told to love his Father. How well St. Augustine put it: "Love, and do what you please." Freedom *from* the law means freedom *for* others.

The disciple of Christ may know the Ten Commandments, the six traditional precepts of the church, the whole network of rules and regulations governing moral behavior, in the way that a good lawyer knows his law books, but he does not live by these laws. He lives by the life of the Master. Christianity is not an ethical code. It is a love affair, a Spirit-filled way of living aimed at making us professional lovers of God and people. To continue to eye God primarily in terms of laws, obligations and town ordinances represents a retreat to a pre-Christian level of thought and a rejection of Jesus Christ and the total sufficiency of His redeeming work.

As church history abundantly proves, one-sided emphasis on the courthouse has domesticated Christian freedom, "Churchified" Jesus, distorted the Gospel into a dull, drab affair and made a mirage of the freedom and glory of the children of God. The call of freedom is changed into the call of a religious party.

Unbalanced emphasis on law has made the church a haven for the shallow and the selfish. It has fostered phariseeism by its heavy stress on doctrinal orthodoxy and cultic regularity rather than on the loving quality of His everyday presence in the workaday world. The mayor of a small town in Alabama is outraged that a nineteen-year-old girl entered church on Sunday in Bermuda shorts. For seven years he has been silent on the issue of racial equality. On Ash Wednesday in a Cleveland restaurant a Catholic woman scrupulously examines her soup to detect the slightest particle of meat but is rude, coarse, arrogant and high-handed with the waitress.

Under the landslide of law, creative Christian conduct has been smothered. There is little desire to transcend the Ten Commandments, which merely mark the threshold of the Christian life. Law has promoted the niggling observance of the bare minimum. Once I received a letter from a thirty-year-old seminarian who had been a bartender for nine years before entering the seminary. By common standards it was a silly, dumb, rambling letter. But between the lines he was crying out, "Please write

53

back. I've got to have someone to talk to." For me not to have written, I believe, would have been sinful.

A pioneering moral theologian named Bernard Haring made an important distinction between the *kronos* and the *kairos*. The *kronos* is measurable time, clock time; the *kairos* is the unique, existential saving *now*. What is the Spirit of Jesus asking of me at this particular moment in these unique circumstances? The external law cannot express the totality of my relationship with God because it was legislated for all people. It cannot take account of individual differences because it does not recognize the parable of the talents, the varying abilities of men and women. It was not the external law that impelled the Kansas City Chiefs' running back Joe Delaney to dive into a lake to rescue a drowning child at the cost of his own life. It was not the external law that caused astronaut John Glenn not to answer the doorbell and receive a prestigious visit from President Lyndon Johnson because his wife, sick in bed, needed his undivided attention. It was not the external law that drove the Good Samaritan to stop and attend to the needs of his bleeding brother, while the priest and Levite, because the external law did not require them to stop, passed him by. Nor was it law that sent an attractive, intelligent twenty-year-old girl from the country-club set in Connecticut to martyrdom as a nun in El Salvador. It is only the Spirit of Jesus, the Spirit of love and compassion that speaks in the *kairos*.

Legalism and moralism, the twin spirits of the settlers, have undermined the community dimension of Christianity. They delude me into believing my relationship with God is strictly a private affair. Exchanging the sign of peace during the liturgy is not only a nuisance: It constitutes an invasion of my privacy. I am neither responsible for nor responsible to others. Religion is kind of a telephone booth affair—an exclusive communication between God and me that has no reference to my brothers and sisters. I go to church and the world can go to hell. I look on as a man is being mugged or a woman is being raped and refuse to intervene because civil law does not hold me accountable.

When hanging around the courthouse drugs me into such insensitivity that I no longer hear the anguished cry of my brother, then Karl Marx was right—religion is the opium of the people.

John Shea, a priest from Chicago, reminisces about his first awareness of the Holy Spirit in his life. He was thirteen years old and an altar boy in his home parish. He and another boy were assigned to meditate for a half hour on the elements of Holy Communion in the sanctuary. John sat down, his eyes roaming around the church. Several times he peeked at his wristwatch. Then he glanced up at the host—the Communion wafer—in its container on the altar. Without speaking the host said, *I'm more than a piece of bread, you know.* John turned immediately and looked at the other altar boy. He was a fat kid with big ears. Everybody in school made fun of him. Without speaking the boy said, *I'm more than a fat kid with floppy ears, you know.*

At the end of the thirty minutes, John left the church. It was dark. On the corner he saw an old woman with a cane waiting to cross the street. She glanced at him and without speaking said, *I'm more than a wrinkled old widow, you know.* John looked up at the sky. The heavens thundered, *I'm more than the sky, you know.*

John Shea's first experience of the Spirit of Jesus brought him to look beyond appearances, beyond size, shape, color, ethnic background, denominational affiliation. It moved him from his ego-self, which made the judgment, *People are only what I think they are and nothing more,* to his Spirit-self, which saw others through the eyes of Jesus— flawed but good, lovable not because of what they do but

55

because of who they are, children of God, his brothers and sisters in the human family. The Spirit also led John into a new appreciation of himself and led him to pray in the words of Psalm 139, "I thank You, Lord, for the wonder of myself."

The Spirit of the settlers with their overriding preoccupation with law has made the institutional church largely irrelevant. What is the effect of the church's presence on the world? Intellectually, politically, culturally and economically, we live in a secular society. The church is two thousand years old, and the world is only 17 percent Christian.

The visible church has an abundance of settlers who know all the facts of salvation. But do they know Jesus? Do *we* know Him? Isn't this the real plight of the church today—that Jesus Christ has been unknown through Christian preaching and worship? Ought we not demolish the walls of the courthouse so as to get back to Him ourselves and to make Him known to others? Would not the cynics, skeptics and the defeated find Jesus thrilling, aggravating and liberating if they could only get sight of Him? If His call to freedom under the Word were sounded, wouldn't this be a new Pentecost from which the Spirit would flow out over the earth?

"Christianity hasn't been tried and found wanting," wrote G. K. Chesterton. "It has been found difficult and left untried." Mahatma Gandhi once said, "I like your Christ but I don't like your Christians." He gave as his reason, "They are so unlike your Christ." Unless and until we have pioneers who respond to the call of freedom, who live by the inner dynamism of the Spirit, human torches aglow with the fire of love for Christ, the Christianity of the courthouse will remain a musty antique from a medieval past.

What a strange breed of Christianity the law has ushered in, and what little resemblance it bears to the Good News of Jesus Christ!

The community formed by Jesus was empowered by God's Word untrammeled by all the later conventional Christian fetters. It is the school of freedom where the language of love is spoken and only the daring need apply. It is the home of free men and women who are a jarring, jolting and disturbing influence on our Christian commitment. The Spirit escapes human categories. St. Augustine said that the Ten Commandments are but a coat hanger on which to hang the radical requirements of the New Law.

What is the best outward expression of the law of the Spirit? We take a clue from Jesus' farewell address in the Upper Room on Holy Thursday where He gave love primacy, saying, "This is the 'new' commandment: that you love one another as I have loved you."

Let us make the requirements of love specific. Have I:

1. Missed the message of the beatitude "Blessed are the peacemakers"? Have I failed to take the initiative in working for social justice on a local level and the end of the nuclear nightmare?
2. Had habitual contempt for others: less educated people, people of different ethnic, racial, economic or religious groups?
3. Dismissed senior citizens as medieval? Never tried to make them feel their worth as persons?
4. In any way stifled the personal development of another? When I sailed for Europe to live with the Little Brothers of Jesus seventeen years ago, my family and friends threw a little farewell party on the ship. About thirty-five people came. One was a nun who began humming a popular song. There was a band aboard ship, and the bandleader heard the nun and asked if she would sing with the musicians. Since she was extremely shy, I encouraged her, telling her what a remarkable gift she had.

She sang a medley of three songs: "The Impossible Dream," "I Believe" and "Climb Every Mountain." When she finished she was offered a job on the spot at $2,000 a week. The bandleader said he had not heard a voice like hers except at the Metropolitan Opera. You know, in twenty-seven years of religious life, that woman had never been asked by her community to sing even an offertory hymn. Sometimes, my brothers and sisters, words *are* deeds.

5. Sought to be respected without respecting others?
6. Often kept others waiting?
7. Carelessly forgotten or not kept a date?
8. Been difficult for others to reach or too busy to put myself at their disposal?
9. Not paid attention to the person speaking to me?
10. Kept silent when I should have spoken out? "We do not have the right to be silent sentinels," wrote Charles de Foucauld. "We must cry out when we see evil being done."
11. Responded only to those whose friendship might prove profitable?
12. Blackened the character of anyone by harmful remarks, false or true?
13. Betrayed a trust, violated a confidence, involved myself in others' affairs through indiscreet words and actions?

And last: Having failed to make an adequate response to this examination of conscience, will I be gentle with myself (as the Master is), humbly acknowledge that the Word has not taken sovereign possession of my life, accept my own need for further conversion and smile at my own frailty?

The Scout on horseback suddenly stops; He turns around, tall in the saddle, and cries out to the wagon train in a powerful voice: "I have set you free and I want you to remain free. Don't turn back!"

FOR REFLECTION

Begin with five minutes of silent prayer, becoming aware in faith of God's indwelling presence and humbly asking the Spirit to speak to your heart through Scripture, personal reflection and the insights of others.

Let one of the group read aloud 2 Corinthians 3:17. Then focus on the following questions for personal reflection and group interaction.

1. A Christian is always in the process of becoming one. Are you experiencing greater freedom from the bondage of human respect, people pleasing and craving the approval of others?
2. Are you taking advantage of a mentor, a guide or a spiritual director to lead you into greater freedom?
3. Share your response to the examination of conscience at the end of this chapter.

CHAPTER 4

The Affluent Poor

A while back, I participated in a five-day directed retreat at the Cenacle on the shores of Lake Pontchartrain near my home in New Orleans.

I got to my room around six at night, dropped my bag on the bed and wondered, *Why did I come here?* With the luxury of a five-day vacation in my lap and all the charming, exciting, delightful places to play—the French Quarter, the beaches of the Mississippi Gulf Coast, the antebellum charm of Vicksburg and Natchez—why did I decide to come to this remote hamlet on the lake with no radio, television or newspaper?

I didn't have to come. I wanted to, I chose to, I preferred the pleasure of Jesus' company to the transitory pleasure of a host of other attractions. Why? Why am I not satisfied with what seems to satisfy so many?

The word that leapt into my mind was *lagniappe*—a bit of Cajun folklore and language that means "something extra." You can't buy it, earn it, merit it or deserve it. It is simply given. For example, if a waiter in the restaurant comes up after dinner and serves a liqueur or a praline pecan sundae and says, "Compliments of the house," that's lagniappe.

St. Augustine taught long ago that Christ was not only the Way but the impulse for us to walk along the way. The desire for silence and solitude, the hunger to be alone with Jesus, is lagniappe—the gratuitous gift of a gracious God.

On the first full day of the retreat, my spiritual director, an old, wise and battle-scarred priest, gave me a bottle of wonder bubbles (with a magic wand), a box of crayons and the passage from Matthew 18 about becoming a little child lost in awe and wonder.

I had made grandiose plans as to what this retreat would be—well structured, minimum of five hours of daily prayer, lengthy meditation of the Scriptures, deeper insight into the person of Jesus—lofty expectations of *felt* intimacy with God. On that first day I couldn't connect two thoughts about God. I was restless. I quit trying to pray because it seemed so artificial. I was left blowing bubbles and doodling with my crayons.

Becoming a little child meant becoming aware that all is gift, that I am helpless and powerless to add a single inch to my spiritual stature. Without the subjective awareness of utter dependence, the personal consciousness of a dynamism outside of self at work in us, I seriously question whether anyone has made real progress in the spiritual life.

So the first movement of the retreat was getting in touch with the basic truth about the human condition: To be human is to be poor. It was tasting what it is like to be powerless. It is painful to be in desolation and darkness, not to be able to control, manage and manipulate

God into letting me experience His loving presence and compassionate care.

The first step in solitude is to divest ourselves of our preconceived ideas of what a retreat should be like. Our unrealistic expectations are grist for the mills of neurosis: "What am I doing wrong? Why can't I find God?" We get so busy deciding what advice to give God about how to relate to us, so set in our needs and expectations, that we are unable to hear God's voice in the messages He is sending us right now. Our prayer becomes merely an expression of our own illusions.

Becoming a little child means celebrating reality, abandoning ourselves to what is. When I was a little boy playing stickball on the street in Brooklyn, I literally would not hear my mother call out the window to me because I was so caught up in the now. Children don't try to control reality: They embrace what is. Our expectations are always fallacies, whether it be what our children should become, what old age should be like, the way other people should respond to us or what direction a retreat should take. All are attempts to control reality and manipulate mystery. We presume that *we* know what is in our best interest.

Are we really aware of how poor we are?

Have you ever awakened in the middle of the night startled by the emptiness of a dark room and terrified by the prospect that one night will have to be the last night of your life? Have faces paraded before your mind's eye, some belonging to people already dead, some you haven't seen for a long time, some very close and dear? Have you ever shivered at the thought that people who are now so important and loved must also pay their dues to the devouring Sister Death? No horror movie has ever had an ending so sure and dreadful. Death is fearsome, and it seems to let loose its worst assaults in the middle of the night.

To calm our fears, we might turn on a lamp or radio or count the number of hours 'til daylight. We might want to pray but often our aloneness, sharpened by fear, shatters our prayer into syllables and all we can manage is to cry out to God for help.[1]

But does He listen? Who has ever seen or touched Him? Does God have a clearly discernible voice? Even as words of gratitude start to form on our lips for an answered prayer, the mind sometimes starts to wonder, *Was anyone ever "there" in the first place?* When an alcoholic or drug addict gets free and flowers into a person who is deeply thankful, pure in spirit, openhearted to the point of being vulnerable, does any divine eye see this great achievement of human spirit? Does anyone notice that I'm here at the Cenacle?

The late French theologian Henri de Lubac wrote:

Why is it that the mind that has found God still retains or constantly reverts to the feeling of not having found Him? Why does His absence weigh on us even in the presence itself, however intimate it may be? Why face to face with Him who penetrates all things, why that insurmountable obstacle, that unbridgeable gap? Why always a wall or a gaping void? Why do all things, as soon as they have shown Him to us, betray us by concealing Him again?

To some people, these reflections may appear to be lack of faith. They suggest uncertainty and fear where religions should be demonstrating conviction and power.

I believe that questions like these reveal how terribly poor the human spirit is. There is so much about ourselves, about where we come from and where we are heading, about our deepest motives, about the purity and sincerity of our prayer, that escapes our comprehension.[2]

When we agonize with the families of the twenty-one persons slaughtered at that fast-food restaurant in San Ysidro, California, with the families of the MIA's in Vietnam, when we agonize over hands without work, stomachs without food, human beings without human rights, we learn why poor people put their trust in God because, finally, there is nothing else.

The awareness of our innate poverty, that we were created from the clay of the earth and the kiss of God's mouth, that we came from dust and shall return to dust, pulls away the mask of prestige, of knowledge, of social class or of strength—whatever it is we use to command attention and respect. (I shudder as I think how often I have worn the clerical collar to serve these very purposes and commanded deference not because of who I was but because of the clothes I wore.) Poverty of spirit breaks through our human pretenses and frees us from the shabby sense of spiritual superiority and the need to stand well with persons of importance.

Poverty brings us to the awareness of the sovereignty of God and our absolute insufficiency. We simply cannot do anything alone. Any growth or progress in the spiritual life cannot be traced to our paltry efforts. All is the work of grace. We cannot even acknowledge that Jesus is Lord except through the gift of the Holy Spirit. Life is lagniappe. We are faced with the possibility of genuine humility. I am convinced that without a gut-level experience of our profound spiritual emptiness, it is not possible to encounter the living God.

It was more than a passing coincidence that the first Scripture reading at the liturgy on the opening day of the retreat was from Micah 6:6–8:

With what shall I come before the LORD and bow down before the exalted God? Shall I come before him with burnt offerings, with calves a year old? Will the LORD be pleased with thousands of rams, with ten thousand rivers of oil? Shall I offer my firstborn for my transgression, the fruit of my body for the sin of my soul? He has showed you, O man, what is good. And what does the LORD require of you? To act justly and to love mercy and to walk humbly with your God.

In the Sermon on the Mount the first words that gushed from Jesus' mouth like a torrent of truth were: "Blessed are the poor in spirit, for theirs is the kingdom of heaven" (Matthew 5:3). The stunning paradox of the affluent poor!

In canonizing the poor in spirit, Jesus reverses all past ideas of human greatness and offers a totally new idea of human vocation. Jesus said in effect: Like a little child consider yourself to be of little account. Blessed are you if you love to be unknown and regarded as nothing: all things being equal, to prefer contempt to honor, to prefer ridicule to praise, to prefer humiliation to glory.

To practice poverty of spirit calls us not to take offense or be supersensitive to criticism. The majority of hurts in our lives, the endless massaging of the latest bruise to our wounded ego, feelings of anger, grudges, resentment and bitterness come from our refusal to embrace our abject poverty, our obsession with our rights, our need for esteem in the eyes of others. If I follow the counsel of Jesus and take the last place, I won't be shocked when others put me there too.

"For whoever exalts himself will be humbled, and whoever humbles himself will be exalted" (Matthew 23:12).

Luke tells us that "at that time Jesus, full of joy through the Holy Spirit, said, 'I praise you, Father, Lord of heaven and earth, because you have hidden these things from the wise and learned, and revealed them to little children'" (Luke 10:21).

Peter writes in his first letter: "Clothe yourselves with humility toward one another, because, 'God opposes the proud but gives grace to the humble.' Humble yourselves, therefore, under God's mighty hand, that he may lift you up in due time" (1 Peter 5:5b–6).

These words are both frightening and consoling. God resists, refuses, rejects the proud. But He delivers Himself up, He gives Himself totally to the humble and the little. Not only does He not resist them, but He cannot refuse them anything. The story of the Canaanite woman in Matthew 15:21–28 is a shining example. "Yes, Lord," she said to Jesus when He pointed out that His mission was to Israel alone, "but even the dogs eat the crumbs that fall from their masters' table." She humbled herself and Jesus exalted her. "Woman, you have great faith! Your request is granted."

Jesus couldn't resist the humility of this foreign woman, of the good thief, of Mary Magdalene.

When my insecurities, low self-esteem and negative self-image lead me to subtle boasting about my accomplishments, when I wax eloquent about the incomparable beauty and extraordinary unity of my marriage or the fantastic achievements of my children, when I try to impress others with the range of my knowledge and the depth of my prayer life, all the while giving lip service to the power of the Holy Spirit, I am directing your attention to myself and stealing from Jesus.

"Without me," Jesus said, "you can do nothing." The humble Christian echoes the cry of Mary in her Magnificat, "He has been mindful of the humble state of his servant. . . . The Mighty One has done great things for me" (Luke 1:48–49).

Throughout my sojourn in solitude at the Cenacle, Jesus was saying, "Walk humbly with your God." Life in the Spirit is lagniappe. Even after the most heroic act of generosity, you can truthfully say, "I am an unprofitable servant." The gate that is truly narrow but accessible to all is that of humility. The narrow way, the narrow gate, is for those who become like little children again. "Whoever humbles himself like this child is the greatest in the kingdom of heaven" (Matthew 18:4).

Children have no past. They abandon themselves to the reality of the present moment. The one who is child-like is not surprised that he often stumbles. He picks himself up again without discouragement, each time more determined to get where he's going.

Being like a little child during the retreat meant fall-ing on my face. (I did that literally one afternoon while I was out jogging by the lake. I was two miles from the Cenacle when the heavens opened. I slipped on the path, went sprawling into the mud, got up looking like a dirt-ball, laughed and kept going.) It meant letting go of my expectations of some mountaintop experience. It meant abandoning myself to what was really happening. And if that was darkness, desolation, aridity and an utter inability to pray—that too was a loving gift from the Father's hand. The Lord knows infinitely better than I what is best for me, and all things, even our sins, St. Augustine said, work together for the good of those who love God.

Concretely, abandonment consists in seeing the will of God in all the people, events and circumstances pres-ent to you. If God tears up your beautiful game plan and leads you into a valley instead of onto a mountaintop, it is because He wants you to discover *His* plan, which is more beautiful than anything you or I could have dreamed up. The response of trust is "Thank You, Jesus," even if it is said through clenched teeth.

One of the greatest paradoxes of the Gospel is that surrender is victory. "The man who loses his life finds it." What makes surrender difficult is our lack of faith, our fears and insecurities, our need to manage our own lives and those of others, our little plans to which we cling so tightly.

In that remarkable discourse in Matthew 6, Jesus says, "Do not worry about your life, what you will eat or drink; or about your body, what you will wear. . . . Seek first his kingdom and his righteousness, and all these things will be given to you as well" (vv. 25, 33).

Often that is what we do not do. We seek first our advantage, best interest, prosperity, whatever. When I blew into the Cenacle, I was not seeking first the Kingdom but what I thought was best for me, and Jesus turned away.

Yet His turning away was not rejection but an invitation to follow Him to a place where I did not want to go. And that place was down a deep well to experience my sinfulness, brokenness and powerlessness in a way I had never known before. Whether taking a shower, jogging on the levee, eating a meal or praying the Scriptures, a vivid recollection of some sin of my past life would flash through my mind. One afternoon I dove under the covers trying to hide from myself. I felt unclean, like a moral leper scarred with sin.

The same night I read a passage from a book by Nikos Kazantzakis, *Letters to Greco*. An old man lies dying. He is filled with grief, remorse and guilt because of his sinful life. At length he dies and goes naked and trembling before the Lord for judgment. Jesus has a big bowl of aromatic oil at his fingertips. He dips a sponge into the sweet-smelling ointment and washes the man clean of his grime and shame. Then Jesus says, "Don't bother me with that stuff anymore. Go over and play."

Suddenly I was filled with peace. The compassion of Jesus enabled me to be compassionate toward myself. A sense of tremendous release and relief swept over me. Involuntarily I was smiling. Then something remarkable happened. Faces of people I knew passed before my eyes: faces of people whom I found irritating, rude, self-centered and downright obnoxious. A tremendous surge of compassion and sympathy for their emptiness, unpleasant personality traits and character defects welled up inside me. My eyes filled with tears. I wanted to carry their burdens. On my way home from the retreat I was riding the ferry from town to the West Bank when I saw an extremely fat and homely woman in her mid-twenties who had probably never once in her life experienced a look of admiration or interest from a man. I wanted to become her, to walk in her obesity and taste her feelings of rejection. I wanted her to see the look of tenderness Jesus gives her simply because she counts for nothing, because she is ignored and rejected by people who attach such importance to physical beauty. I wanted her to accept the love of Jesus Christ and be so filled with joy that all the human neglect and contempt would not rob her of her dignity.

What the Lord showed me at the Cenacle was this: Before I am asked to show compassion toward my brothers and sisters in their suffering, He asks me to accept His compassion in my own life, to be transformed by it, to become caring and compassionate toward myself in my own suffering and sinfulness, in my own hurt, failure and need. The degree of our compassion for others depends upon our capacity for self-acceptance. When I am most unhappy with myself, I am most critical of others. When I am most into self-condemnation, I am most judgmental of others. It is a truism that the saints, like Christ, are the most unjudgmental of Christians. They get on very well with sinners. They are not severe with human weaknesses or those addicted to sins of the flesh. (Also, like Jesus, they are not lenient with those guilty of religious hypocrisy.)

When the compassion of Christ is interiorized, made personal and appropriated to ourselves, the breakthrough into caring for others occurs. In the mystery of divine wholeness, the way of compassionate caring for others brings healing to ourselves, and compassionate caring for ourselves brings healing to others. Solidarity with human suffering frees the one who receives it and liberates the one who gives it through the conscious awareness "I am the other."

Whether it be a lakeside retreat or the journey of life, our expectations are our greatest obstacle to union with God in the present moment. It is Jesus who writes all the lines, all the words and all the letters of our lives. Do I really know what is best for me? My vision is so short-sighted, my horizon so limited. *Surrender* is a practical application of a confession—what we pray each day in the Lord's Prayer, "Thy will be done." Abandonment is the triumph of trust in our lives.

In days long ago when there were no spiritual directors or brilliant commentaries on Scripture, fidelity to God's will was the whole of spirituality. The two pivotal words in the teaching of Jesus are both *A* words—*amen* and *Abba, amen* meaning *yes* and *Abba* meaning *Father.* Saying yes to our heavenly Father's will is the essence of the entire moral teaching of Jesus. God will bring good out of evil—even a greater good than if there had been no evil—and the trial will have been an immense good for us.

The prophet Jeremiah is a striking example of the biblical paradox that surrender means victory, that in losing our life we find it. (Jesus Christ identifies with Jeremiah more than any other prophet and quotes him most frequently.) In the year 625 B.C., the Lord summoned Jeremiah to a prophetic career. Jeremiah's immediate response was reluctance. "Ah, Lord God," he said, "I know not how to speak. I am too young." (He was nineteen at the time.) Jeremiah was not the confident, self-assured type like Amos or Isaiah. Sensitive, accustomed to the quiet of small-town life, he was temperamentally unsuited for public life and the harsh treatment that is the customary "reward of the prophets."

Timid and afraid, Jeremiah had no ambition for such a mission. In no way did he want to preach God's Word to his fellow Israelites. Nothing pleased him more than to be Mr. Nobody, ignored by the ruling clique of royal counselors and priests. How content he would have been to live in the tiny world of his own heart. And so he remonstrated with God, "Ah, Lord God, I am only a boy." Each of us can sympathize, because Jeremiah is Everyman and Everywoman.

On our wedding day or ordination day or the day of our baptism in the Spirit, bells of joy ring out. Hearts bubble with enthusiasm. The hymn of thanksgiving is sung. Surely it will continue forever.

But sometimes life muffles the hymn. Perhaps the scandal of someone's bad example becomes an excuse for demanding that much less of myself. The Christian life may stretch through an arid land of trifling necessities and day-by-day routine. The whisper of temptation can be loud: "Why did God bring me here? Why not someplace else?" Marriage may turn into the doldrums of petty jobs, the frustration of doing things that never stay done. Jeremiah is Everyman and Everywoman: What God wants done clashes with what I want to do for Him.

This rebellion against God's will expresses itself in different ways: We become jealous, develop inferiority complexes, inflict our anger on others through moodiness, revenge or despondency. Envy invades the mind of a person when he sees that another has succeeded where he has failed. The family next door has none of my troubles, and yet they never thank God for His gifts, while my home is plagued with sickness and troubles and doctor bills despite my prayers. From the seed of envy grows the flower of discontent: "If only I could be that other person rather than the person God has made me." From discontent grows despair: "I fail so often. What's the use of trying?" To us, as He did to Jeremiah (1:8, JB), God is saying at each moment of the day, "Do not be afraid. I am with you to protect you." The loving acceptance of the Father's will kindles a fire within us that burns away envy and lights up our despondency and despair.

> Reactions of anger, moodiness, or revenge are actually manifestations of a hidden revolt against God's Providence. Like a small child unable to control the actions of a grownup, we stomp our feet and pout in a corner. Once again our actions are speaking to God louder than words: "Why didn't you arrange it differently?" In chapter 30, verse 24, Jeremiah draws his strength from the reassuring promise of God: "In days to come, you will understand this."
>
> These words of God are enough for any person of faith. Like the mighty theme of a symphony, Jeremiah hears God saying, "I am with you to deliver you." The saints have understood God's plan. Often, when St. Paul of the Cross met with trouble and contradiction, he doffed his little skull cap, bowed his head and whispered, "Thy Will be done."[3]

Jeremiah reminds us that a vocation is whatever God wants. It is accepting ourselves just as He made us, with our talents, disposition and character, or the lack of them. God may give us one talent for teaching and five talents for compassion. His demands may be so ordinary, so common, that they stir little response in our emotions. Yet in God's will alone can we find peace. Even though hidden from us, following God's will can only mean success. The prophet Jeremiah is a shining example of a successful failure.

For many of us, trust does not come easily. Trust does not come from discovering in philosophy or cosmology some proof that God exists. Sometimes it happens when my eyes meet yours or when we share something in common. It is most likely to happen if I love you. Ultimately we trust God because we love Him. Not the other way around: not trust first, then love. Job trusted because he loved.

You will trust God only as much as you love Him. And you will love Him not because you have studied Him; you will love Him because you have touched Him—in response to His touch. Even then your troubles are not over. You may still wrangle with God. You may cry out with Jesus, "My God, my God, why have You forsaken me?" Only if you love will you make that final leap into darkness: "Father, into Your hands I commend my spirit."

A priest from the Bahamas related this episode. A two-story house caught fire. The family—father, mother, several children—were on their way out when the smallest boy became terrified and ran back upstairs. Seconds later he appeared at a smoke-filled window. His father, outside, shouted to him: "Jump, son, jump! I'll catch you." The boy cried: "But, Daddy, I can't see you." "I know," his father called, "I know. But I can see you."

As the retreat at the lakeside came to an end, I prayed with greater trust than in the past, "Thank You, Jesus, for everything—including my alcoholism. It took every drop I drank and every shame I endured to bring me to where I am today, and I would not change it. Thank You for the rejection, contempt and desertion that have come from some people because of my marriage. You have used them, Lord, to set me free from people-pleasing and the desire to be thought well of by everyone."

I believe Jesus calls all of us to let go of the desire to appear good, to give up the appearance of being good, so that we can listen to the word within us and move in the mystery of who we are. The preoccupation with projecting the perfect image, with being a model Christian and edifying others with our virtues, leads to self-consciousness, sticky pedestal behavior and bondage to human respect.

As my director Larry Hein said, paraphrasing the Tao de Ching, "Give up being a saint. It'll be a lot better for everybody."

Larry has a poster on the wall of his room, beautifully lettered by a retreatant who heard him speak these words in a counseling session: "We must let go of everything we have taken literally all our lives and find our own symbols. Only then will we be open to the mystery of God within us." In New Orleans, a gay rights ordinance that would give homosexuals equal opportunity for employment and housing was soundly defeated—largely by the fierce opposition of the hierarchy of the Roman Catholic Church. If we are using the Gospel to segregate gays, batter blacks, justify prejudice toward Hispanics, Asians, Jews or any of God's children, then get rid of the Gospel so that we may experience the Gospel. If God is invoked to justify division, competition, contempt and hatred among Christian sects in the Body of Christ and hostility toward other world religions, then get rid of God so that we may find God. As the fourteenth-century mystic Meister Eckhart said: "I pray that I may be quit of God that I may find God." Our closed human concepts of Gospel and God can prevent us from experiencing both and stifle our freedom to love one another in a nonjudgmental way.

Let me make a suggestion. Each day take a little time to pause and pray, "Jesus, I thank You for everything."

In this simple prayer there is humility, a deep trust in His love, surrender and thanksgiving. It glorifies Jesus and pleases the Father. It is a cry of abandonment. Actually, it is nothing more than what Paul asked of the Ephesians in chapter 5, verse 20: "Always and everywhere giving thanks to God who is our Father in the name of our Lord Jesus Christ" (JB).

As you pray daily in this way, I believe you will hear the Father say something like this:

75

My child, fan the flame of your confidence in Me. Keep it burning. I want you to be happy, to come back again and again to this feeling of trust until you are never without it. Trust is an aspect of love. If you love Me and believe in My love for you, you will surrender your whole self into My hands like a little child who doesn't even ask, "Where are you taking me?" but sets off joyously, hand in hand with his mother. How many blessings this happy confidence wins for you, My little one.

Keep going blindly. Take delight in knowing nothing about the future. I know how to lead the blind by the best paths. And when this blind person knows that he is My son, she is My daughter, won't they be glad of their infirmity, since it has power over My heart? In all this see My tenderness. It is everlasting.

FOR REFLECTION

Begin with five minutes of silent prayer, becoming aware in faith of God's indwelling presence and humbly asking the Spirit to speak to your heart through Scripture, personal reflection and the insights of others.

Let one of the group read aloud Matthew 5:1–3. Then focus on the following questions for personal reflection and group interaction.

1. What does it mean to you to disappear into the tremendous poverty that is the adoration of God?
2. Are you able to receive the compassion of Jesus, be compassionate with yourself and pass it on to others? If not, why not?
3. What does Meister Eckhart mean when he says, "I pray that I may be quit of God that I may find God"?

JESUS
AT EASTER

———

CHAPTER 5

Showdown
in the Spirit

T he daily newspaper of New Orleans, the *Times-Picayune,* carried a front-page article on the dramatic growth of a nondenominational church in the area that has burgeoned from 250 to 2,500 members in the past few years. What caught my eye was a remark of a wealthy member of the congregation. Photographed in the ornate restaurant that he owns, surrounded by sprinkling fountains, this man said that his faith in God has made him hugely successful, financially as well as spiritually. "It's not an automatic ticket to success," he conceded, "but man, if you don't find success in God, you haven't found God." He claims that he and other members have found their incomes doubling and tripling "as a direct result of God blessing us."

I hope that you are as profoundly disturbed as I am by this new definition of "successful" Christianity. Do you get the uncomfortable feeling that God is being used? The

. self-centeredness of our culture spawns a self-centered religion. The most common question in evangelism today is, "What can Jesus do for me?" Potential converts are told that Jesus can make them happier, better adjusted and more prosperous. Jesus quickly becomes the supreme product, attractively packaged and aggressively sold to a consuming public. Everywhere you turn there are billboards, buttons and bumper stickers—"Honk if you love Jesus." He's being advertised in a competitive market with every ingenious Madison Avenue sales technique. Even more than Coca-Cola, Jesus is "the real thing."

As Jim Wallis notes in *The Call to Conversion:*

> The Gospel message is being molded to suit an increasingly narcissistic culture. Conversion is proclaimed as the road to self-realization . . . religion . . . as a way to help us uncover our human potential—our potential for personal, social and business success, that is. Modern conversion brings Jesus into our lives rather than bringing us into his. We are told that Jesus is here to help us do better what we are already doing. Jesus doesn't change our lives, he improves them.[1]

What a tragic distortion of the Gospel! Christianity is made compatible with the worship of other gods. Christ is used to serve the interests of wealth and power. Listening to some evangelical preachers, you would never get the idea that the coming of Jesus was intended to turn the world upside down.

In entering human history God shattered all previous conceptions of who God is and what people are meant to be. In the New Testament we are presented with a God who suffers crucifixion, a Supreme Being with spit on his face. What He went through in His passion and death is meant for me too; the invitation He issues is, "Don't weep for Me! Join Me! The life I have planned for Christians is a Christian life, much like the life I led. I wasn't poor so that you might be rich. I wasn't mocked so that you might be honored. I wasn't laughed at so that you could be lauded. I was revealing the Christian picture of man and woman, one that is meant to include you too." Paul wrote to the Colossians, "We are meant to fill up what is wanting in the suffering of Christ."

Modern evangelism's preoccupation with a triumphal Savior and a prosperity Gospel makes the crucifixion an insignificant cipher, or as Jürgen Moltmann says, "a mere theological necessity for the process of salvation." We get so used to the ultimate Christian fact—Jesus stripped, flogged and crucified—that we no long see Him for what He actually is: a living injunction to strip ourselves of earthly cares and worldly wisdom, all desire for human praise, greediness for any kind of comfort, spiritual consolations included; a living summons to let go of every kind of worldliness—including that which prefers the more attractive duty to the less attractive, which prods us to put more effort into relationships with the people we want to stand well with. Even the last rag we cling to—the self-flattery that suggests that we are being rather humble when we disclaim any resemblance to Jesus Christ—even that rag has to go when we stand face-to-face with the crucified Son of Man.

The legalistic distortion of the Gospel erects a protective screen of piety between the worshiper and that life-changing encounter. It ensures that the Word of God no longer rustles like refreshing rain on the parched ground of our souls. It no longer sweeps like a wild storm into the comfortable corners of our well-fed virtue. The Gospel becomes just a pattering of pious platitudes spoken by a Jewish carpenter in the distant past.

A case in point: When Jesus, the new Moses, climbed the mountain to deliver His inaugural address, He began

His sermon with the words, "Blessed are the poor in spirit: the kingdom of heaven is theirs." The Christ of God reverses all past ideas of human greatness and brings a totally new idea of human vocation. He said in effect: Blessed are you if you love to be overlooked and regarded as nothing. The Be-attitudes, as John Powell calls them, these attitudes of being, spell out the game plan for a radically different lifestyle of constant prayer, total unselfishness, buoyant, creative goodness and unbridled involvement in the material and spiritual well-being of God's children.

Small wonder that C. S. Lewis, after reading the Beatitudes, remarked:

> A man who was merely a man and said the sort of things Jesus said would not be a great moral teacher. He would either be a lunatic—on a level with the man who says he is a poached egg—or else he would be the Devil of Hell. You must make your choice. You can fall at his feet and call him Lord and God. But let us not come with any patronizing nonsense about his being a great human teacher. He has not left that open to us. He did not intend to.[2]

For the most part the poor do not see the evangelicals today as their allies. Rather, many evangelicals are known to have a decided preference for the successful and prosperous who see their wealth, like the restaurant owner I mentioned, as a sign of God's blessing and favor. Wittingly or unwittingly, they lay a guilt trip on the sick and the unemployed, on all those of us who do not enjoy power, progeny, long life and other alleged signs of God's benevolence.

I can think of no other time in history when the name of Jesus has been so frequently mentioned and the content of His life and teaching so thoroughly ignored. When the true prophetic voice is raised in the church, it is never simply to denounce and indict. The prophet undertakes his vocation out of love for the people and a deep desire to see them restored to the Lord. In order to free the captives, the captivity has to be named. And in America, in our day, our captivity is to the prosperity gospel.

The Father calls us to be like His Son, Jesus, to become "another self," for His risen Son. Well, the life of the historical Jesus as presented in the Gospels is largely a life of failure, sorrow, rejection and loneliness before the final victory. On the eve of His death, Jesus had failed to convert anyone, even His own disciples. As He knelt in the Garden of Gethsemane, He was in an agony so intense that His beads of sweat became drops of blood. "My soul," He said, "is ready to die with sorrow." His reproach to Peter, James and John, "Couldn't you watch even an hour with Me?" reveals how on that night Jesus longed for human companionship. The following day, the hallowing cries of acclamation of the previous Sunday turned to harrowing cries of rejection: "Crucify Him!"

Such was the life of Jesus on earth. The Gospels tell of a man who was cut off in the flower of His age, His work destroyed just when it should have taken root, His friends scattered, His honor broken, His name a laughingstock. In the words of Isaiah, He was "a worm and not a man, a thing despised and rejected by men, a man of sorrows and familiar with suffering," who experienced the nadir of an agony such as no other man or woman has ever dreamed of. No one has ever died as Jesus died, because He was life itself. No one was ever punished for sin as He was—the sinless One. No one ever plunged down into the vacuum of evil as did Jesus of Nazareth. Who will ever know the excruciating pain behind His words, "My Father, why have You abandoned Me?"

This is the New Testament picture of Jesus—the suffering servant, a man who lives as a lackey and dies in disgrace. He is spurned, avoided, treated as a leper, a born loser. He is one stricken by God, publicly beaten, whipped by disgusted, righteous society. Eliminate Him, they say; He is distasteful. Drive Him across the tracks, out of town, out of society. He is roughly handled, pushed around, taken out, killed and buried among evildoers.

Jesus never explained the "why" of suffering (though we may never have known the depth of His love if, for example, He had saved us with a smile). He simply made it the indispensable condition for discipleship. Never once did Jesus ask those who wanted to join the company of His friends if they were chaste, honest, sober or respectable. Never once did He attempt to charm anyone to His service with fair promises of happiness. On the contrary, with uncompromising honesty, He said, "If anyone will come after Me, let him take up his cross daily. And whoever does not take up his cross daily (not weekly or monthly) and come after Me cannot be My disciple."

You might suppose that longing for love, as Jesus must have longed, He would have at least encouraged those who came to Him. But to the young man who said, "Jesus, I'll follow You wherever You go," Christ answered in the loneliest words any man has ever uttered: "The foxes have their holes, the birds of the air their nests, but the Son of Man has nowhere to lay His head." In other words, "Friend, if you want to come My way, then be prepared to live My life. And My life is often a life of homeless, wandering sorrow."

This cautionary reminder of Jesus—that those who followed Him would share in the fellowship of His suffering—was certainly not a prosperity Gospel, but neither was it simply a test. It wasn't like the traditional trial in the fairy tale that disappears as soon as the right answer is given. Of the twelve men whom Jesus called in the inner circle of His love, one died by his own hand in despair and all the others were murdered except one, John, who lived on for almost a hundred years enduring the more terrible martyrdom of not being able to lay down his life for Jesus, of living out the years of loneliness without the sight of the beautiful face that once his eyes had seen, without the closeness of that human heart upon which he had once laid his head.

Jesus turned to His own mother and asked her to drink most deeply of the cup of His suffering. On the Friday we call Good, it was Mary beneath that wooden instrument of torture, suffering with Jesus, giving back to God the Son of God. It was Mary holding her dead child in her lap, covering His bloodied brow with her kisses.

In the mystery of Christ's vocation, and those of His mother and friends, the apostle Paul quickly discovered the master clue to his own. Referring to Paul, the Lord told Ananias, "I will show him how much he has to suffer for My name's sake." Through shipwreck, arrests and floggings, Paul learned that suffering was to fill his life.

Through our baptism we were incorporated into Christ. Our Christian vocation is our heavenly Father's invitation to enter into the sufferings of Jesus Christ, to share his life of humiliation, misunderstanding, rejection, loneliness and inevitable victory. Whether we be priest or layperson, housewife or husband, coal miner or research physicist, these are but the life circumstances in which our resemblance to Christ crucified is to be achieved. The Father wills to conform us to the dying state of Jesus. And this is no chance affair. It is the interior law of the Father's purpose. Suffering is not an accident in the Christian life. It is a necessity imposed by divine decree. Confronted with the evidence of Christ's life and the life of the early church, we can say that suffering is the touchstone of the Christian life, and if the cross is not in your life, then it cannot be very Christian.

All the physical suffering in our lives (and here I speak of the suffering ordained by God that is not meant to be submitted to the healing power of Jesus Christ), all the mental anguish, the tension, the contradictions we meet with, the betrayal by enemies, the abandonment by friends, the inability to relate warmly to others—these are the dramatic and more often undramatic life circumstances in which our resemblance to the crucified Christ is accomplished. And the cross of frustration in all its forms:

. . . The outwardly successful marriage, which in reality has become empty of meaning: husband and wife continuing for the sake of appearance, or from a sense of duty, or because of the children, to act as a happy couple while in reality there is no longer any true communion between them or any hope of such.

. . . The men and women who long for married life and never achieve it. Those who have a deep desire to become this or that, to achieve this or that, but in the end have to admit they lack the necessary gifts.

. . . Those who yearn for friends and companionship but seem condemned to loneliness. Those who never seem able to make a real success of anything to which they put their hands. In the moral sphere, those who long to live a good life but feel hopelessly defeated by some vice that they lack the ability to conquer. The frustration that weighs down on all those whose faith, prayer and service to God, having begun with high ideals and generous self-giving, have since become meaningless; faith no longer giving any assurance, any comfort, any drive; prayer and ministry reduced to empty routine lacking any sense of reality.

. . . And the suffering of those who weep when human flesh bleeds and starves and dies; when three million refugees water the road and rice paddies with their tears; when human rights are violated; when people are raped by injustice when there are still countries where to be black is not to be beautiful but bastard; when human beings are tortured by other human beings; when twelve million Russians in a given year are imprisoned in the Gulag Archipelago; when twenty thousand living in the streets of Calcutta build little fires to cook scraps of food, defecate against the curbstones and curl up against a wall to sleep; when alcohol and drugs destroy bodies and souls; when human blood reddens the earth from South Africa to the north of Ireland to the streets of your hometown; when they see the swollen bellies in Ethiopia, the ghetto streets of New York, the decaying schoolhouses in Appalachia.

To these blessed who weep now, the prosperity Gospel has nothing to say. And yet these are the real-life circumstances in which our resemblance to the crucified Christ is daily fleshed out. In what sense can we say this?

Everybody has a vocation to some form of life work. But behind that and deeper than that, everybody has a vocation to be a person, to be fully and deeply a human being, to be Christlike. And the second thing is more important than the first. It is more important to be a great person than a great teacher, butcher or candlestick maker. And if the only chance of succeeding in the second is to fail in the first, the failure, from God's point of view, is fruitful. Won't it be fruitful if it teaches a person to be gentle with the failure of others? Successful, they might have been wrapped up in their own achievements and impatient with the sorrow of others; they might never have come to understand the human heart; they might have come to think of success as their due; and then if their little world had collapsed through some disaster, they would have had no inner resources.

It is through such failure and weeping that the Abba of Jesus conforms us to the image of His Son. Yet if our faith is not alive and dynamically operative, suffering is absurd, pointless. When someone we love meets with a violent accident, when a child is brutally murdered or dies of cancer, when a deep relationship is broken up, when 269 people die as a Korean jetliner is shot out of the sky over Russian territory—when any disappointment or upheaval strikes—despair may set in. Shaking our fists, pounding the air, we ask the futile question, Why, why, why? Most of all, why *me?* What have I done to deserve it? If I were God, I wouldn't allow such awful things to happen. How can there be a God of love when the world is full of suffering? We conclude that either God is cruel, unjust and without mercy, or there is no God and we are adrift in total chaos. It's a classic double bind, a Catch-22 situation. Heads nobody wins, tails we all lose.

Traveling by train one summer, I met an eighty-five-year-old Anglican minister on his way from Canada to Korea to spend the rest of his life teaching grade school. During the trip we had a long conversation. The old man remarked that he met very few Christians anymore, and he prophesied that Russia would be converted before England and America. And then, quite unexpectedly, he said, "You know, young man, I often visit your Catholic churches." When I asked why, he answered, "It's to see the cross with the figure of Christ nailed upon it. There I find the essential fact of Christianity."

The old man's discovery was the same one made by Paul, who, though he preached all the mysteries of Christianity, claimed that he knew but one: "During my stay with you," he wrote to the Corinthians, "the only knowledge I claimed to have was about Jesus, and only about him as the crucified Christ" (1 Corinthians 2:2 JB). In the twenty-first century, the conditions for Christian discipleship remain the same. We must suffer with Him.

We have a beautiful synonym for *baptize* in English, found in no other language, the verb *christen*. It is made up of the noun *Christ* and the Greek suffix *en,* meaning "to make." When you whiten a wall, you make it white.

When you brighten a room, you make it bright. When God christens a person, God makes that person Christ. Christ lives in us, and our sufferings are His passion continuing in the world.

Here we reach the heart of Paul's teaching on Christian suffering: It has its theological roots in our union with Jesus. There is an intimate bond between the sufferings of Christ and the conflict and suffering in each Christian life. The daily dying of the Christian is a prolongation of Christ's own death. Paul writes in Romans 6:3, "Don't you know that all of us who were baptized into Christ Jesus were baptized into his death?" Baptism is not merely a momentary dying; it inaugurates a lifelong *state of death* to the world, to the flesh and to sin. Our daily death to selfishness, dishonesty and degraded love is our personal participation in the fellowship of His sufferings. Years ago, a friend of mine, Peter Lyons, a man steeped in the Word, told me that for him the most meaningful line in all the fourteen letters of Paul is found in Philippians 3:10: "All I want is to know Christ and the power of his resurrection and to share his sufferings by reproducing the pattern of his death" (JB).

The redemptive value of Jesus' suffering lay not in the suffering itself (for in itself it has no value) but in the love that inspired it. On the cross Christ reveals that suffering is a consequence of sin. That does not mean that when I suffer I am necessarily being punished for my sins. Christ was not punished for His. Because we have been plunged into Christ, He continues to live His passion within us. The French poet Paul Claudel put it this way: "Since the incarnation, Jesus has only one desire: to recommence the human life he lived. That's why he wants additional human natures, people who'll let him start all over again." And He needs us to do that. We fill up what is wanting, Paul says, in the suffering of Christ. Thirty-three years wasn't long enough to do all

He meant to do. As Claudel says poetically, "Have pity on him, for all he had was thirty-three years to suffer." A man can only die once. Christ needed to suffer and love in every possible way. But He couldn't love like a woman and He couldn't die the death of an old man; and unless we let Him, many of the things He wished to do will have to go undone.

This teaching is totally Paul. It does not question the total sufficiency of Christ's redeeming work on earth. What it does mean is that as living members of His Body, *our suffering has redemptive significance.* It is not a meaningless torture. The suffering of each of us in Christ Jesus can bring healing to the whole Body. Not that our suffering will dispense others from working out their salvation, but it may win for others the grace to start! How many deathbed conversions can be attributed to Christian mothers and fathers, hidden nuns and monks in contemplative orders, to the aged, the "useless," the suffering members of Christ's Body?

When the shadow of His cross darkens our space and our secure, well-regulated lives are blown apart, when disaster makes its unwelcome appearance in our lives and we are deaf to everything but the shriek of our own misery, when courage flies out the window and the world suddenly seems hostile and menacing, it is the showdown in the Spirit of Jesus.

A woman who has been there, Mary Craig, says:

In the early stages, self-pity is the first, unavoidable, normal, and probably right reaction. I don't see how it's possible to fight self-pity. We only exhaust ourselves by trying to keep it at bay. But there is a time limit, and we alone can fix it. I believe it is possible to recognize the point of no return, the moment when self-pity threatens to become malignant. And that is when we have to stand firm, for if once we allow it to get a real hold we are doomed. . . . However tempting the flight into unreality may be, there is no lasting comfort in it. Fantasy feeds on itself and turns into madness, drug-taking becomes addiction, drinking easily leads to alcoholism. They are blind alleys. The only cure for suffering is to face it head on, grasp it round the neck and use it.[3]

Even in Christian circles, though, the idea of redemptive suffering is not universally accepted. Some leaders teach that suffering is a sign either of a demon or of unrepented sin. Redemptive suffering is nonsense, the bleating of a religious maniac. Yet isn't it possible, as Paul writes, that in the course of time all things work together for the good?

In the concentration camp of Ravensbruck, Germany, that graveyard of human life and longing, an unknown prisoner wrote this prayer on a torn scrap of wrapping paper and left it by the body of a dead child:

O Lord, remember not only the men and women of good will, but also those of ill will. But do not remember the suffering they have inflicted on us; remember the fruits we have born, thanks to this suffering—our comradeship, our loyalty, our humility, our courage, our generosity, the greatness of heart, which has grown out of all this, and when they come to judgment, let all the fruits we have borne be their forgiveness.[4]

In our own showdown, when it's our turn to be broken at the wheel; when we want to run away into drinking, drugging or sexual license; when we want to flee into fantasy or self-pity, there lies the option of acceptance of the cross of Jesus Christ and the possibility of salvation and growth for ourselves and others. We can say to the God of our dark journey, "For what it's worth, here it is. Take it and use it. Use it for the hungry, the homeless, the lonely; for the man down the road who has lost both his job and his wife; for the friend whose little girl has been killed. Use it to help me understand, to be less self-centered, more loving."

We may have to say it with clenched teeth as Jesus did in the Garden of Gethsemane, in doubt and fear but in the full acceptance of what had to be. Is any real knowledge of Jesus possible if we do not experience His sorrow, loneliness and pain? In the neighborhood where I grew up in Brooklyn, there lived an elderly Jewish couple who were always kind to me. One afternoon, sitting on a bench on the boardwalk in Coney Island, the old man said to me: "I love my wife with all my heart, but there is a part of her past that is like a room sealed off. She was in Auschwitz in the forties. She has never spoken about it. After all these years of marriage, I can't say that I really know her." Is any real knowledge of Jesus Christ possible without sharing in the fellowship of His suffering?

My brother or sister, the cross of Jesus not only illumines the enigma of suffering: It is a mighty source of light on every dilemma a human being can face. Let us see how it applies to an immediate, practical and very touchy problem in the world and the church today. Jesus' death on Calvary illustrates better than anything else His lived principle of *not resisting evil*. The fact that evil can be overcome in this fashion is comprehended by very few Christians. And these few, this little band of disciples, are convinced that Jesus presented in His words and in His behavior not only a good way of doing things, not only an ideal to be carried out whenever it is convenient, but the only way of doing what He did. Redemption has come to us in the form of a cross. Suffering love is God's strategy for overcoming evil. His only strategy. God saves through suffering. Charles de Foucauld said, "Not by his words or his works, not even by his miracles, but by his Cross." He overcame evil by surrendering to it in love and obedience.

92

The Christian response to evil—to aggression—is resistance, of course, but nonviolent resistance, the resistance of love, prayer and accepted suffering. When Christians do anything else, they have parted company with Jesus. Nonviolence is the expression of a faith that the greatest power in human history is the forward movement of love. Nonviolence is as realistic as Jesus Himself, and it is one with the cross of Christ's victory over evil. The question of whether or not nonviolent resistance "works" should be referred not so much to the gain of an immediate victory as to the transformation of history from within by the converging forces of love. Gandhi wrote that "Jesus lived and died in vain if he did not teach us to regulate the whole of life by the eternal law of love."

This point has been stressed by Scripture scholar Marcus Barth in his book *Acquittal by Resurrection.* If God so loved the world as to forgive all men and women for the murder of His Son, and to make out of that murder the cause of His murderer's redemption, how can people fail to forgive each other their mutual crimes? What man can serve as the executioner of his brother when God refused to execute those guilty of the death of His Son? After that acquittal, there is no crime on earth, no form of aggression, that can justify a person deliberately taking the life of another.

Pacifism was such a characteristic of the early church that a pagan prince, the Roman Celsus, warned that if everybody became Christian, it would spell disaster for Rome—for the empire would be without military defense! According to church historian William Bausch, there is no clear evidence of Christians serving in the army for the first century and a half of our faith. If they had been in the army, they left after baptism. A partial reason was that a Christian soldier might be forced to engage in emperor worship, but the fear of spilling blood was predominant. Tertullian noted that a Christian would rather be killed than kill. Cyprian, Arnobius, Hippolytus and other church fathers insisted that a soldier must refuse to kill. Later, concerning killing in war, St. Basil the Great said that those who did so should abstain from Holy Communion for a three-year period. Origen added: "Christians should beware lest for warfare . . . we should take out the sword, for no such occasion is allowed by the evangelical teaching." Lactantius said that killing is forbidden in such a way that no exception is to be made.

Yet during the Vietnam War the *Chicago Tribune* ran a comic strip for children, "Tales of the Green Beret," which was syndicated in twenty-five papers across the country. Sample dialogue between two Green Berets: "We kidnap, we burn, we execute . . . we clobber the Vietcong from the inside, where they live. It's cruel, ruthless, the kind of war they invented. They use terrorism, assassination. We're giving it back to them in spades."

We could rejoice when a headline in *The New York Times* proclaimed that *only* two hundred Americans were killed this week. We could be glad when five thousand Vietcong were flushed out and massacred. But these are not statistics to the Lord Jesus; these are persons. And when even one shrieks to heaven with his flesh in flames—friend or enemy—we should all weep, we should all be ashamed.

It will be said that whatever truth there may be in the principle of nonviolent resistance and in the God who gives it meaning, it remains utopian, naive and politically irrelevant. Confronted with the possibility of a nuclear Armageddon, nonviolent resistance has no place.

Yet in the world of politics as in the world of individual conduct, the Christian is not free to let someone else make his or her decisions. We are not free to postpone doing what is right until everyone else has done it before us. Whether we change the popular will and the military stance is not important; what is important is the showdown—whether or not we act according to the Spirit as members of Christ's Body. We need no help from the crowd to do this.

Perhaps the real question is: May the Christian—indeed must the Christian—face the possibility that there are occasions in which there is no Christian way to survive? Do we believe in the invincible power of redemptive suffering? Are there enough women and men of deep faith who are willing to work, suffer and die in spiritual resistance to the inhuman attitudes that are now in control?

Happily, the cross is not the final word that God has spoken to His people. Our Christian lives look beyond Calvary to Resurrection, and it is the human nature of the risen Christ, shot through and through with the radiance of divinity, that shows like a radiant mirror all that we are summoned to. The destiny of Christ our Brother is our destiny. If we have suffered with Him, we shall be glorified with Him. The pattern is always the same. We reach life only through death; we come to light only through darkness; the grain of wheat must fall into the ground and die. Jonah must be buried in the whale's belly.

In the words of the apostle Thomas, "Let us go to Jerusalem and die with Him."

FOR REFLECTION

Begin with five minutes of silent prayer, becoming aware in faith of God's indwelling presence and humbly asking the Spirit to speak to your heart through Scripture, personal reflection and the insights of others.

Let one of the group read aloud Mark 8:34–38. Then focus on the following questions for personal reflection and group interaction.

1. Share the heartache, pain and suffering in your life, whether mental, emotional, physical or spiritual.

2. Have your failures, handicaps and personal grief made you more compassionate toward the failures and shortcomings of others? Give one illustration.

3. A recent national survey revealed that a mere 9 percent of Christians in America evaluated the morality of the war in Iraq in light of the life and teaching of Jesus of Nazareth. The inscription on the bracelet, "What would Jesus do?" has virtually disappeared from Christian conversation. Does your identity in Christ influence your thinking about war? Is the principle of nonviolent resistance relevant in this era of terrorism? What are the alternatives?

CHAPTER 6

The Transparent Disciple

Once upon a time there was a girl named Jackie who lived in the ghetto of a large American city. She never knew her father: Whoever he was, he was never married to her mother. Jackie lived with her mother but never knew a mother's love; her mother was harsh, cruel, brutal. It didn't take Jackie long to discover the truth about the long line of uncles who periodically stayed with them.

Growing up in this kind of jungle, surrounded by bitterness and contempt, Jackie quickly built up a hard shell of self-defense. People were out to get what they could, and if you were in their way, they would trample you.

As she advanced into her teens, she became an object of interest for men. But that was just the trouble: She was merely an object, a source of entertainment. A "Kleenex" girl, they called her, to be used and tossed

JESUS AT EASTER

away. Jackie felt the only way she could survive was to get the world before the world got her. So she tuned out, cut off, closed in.

And then one day in summer she met, quite by chance, a young graduate student who was working in the ghetto as part of his field experience in social work. His background had been much different from hers. He had grown up with love, understanding and trust. Consequently he was a secure man who valued himself not for what he accomplished but just because of who he was. Peter was a warm, loving person.

When he first saw Jackie, he greeted her with a friendly smile, but she gave him one of those if-looks-could-kill glances in return. This didn't put Peter off; he continued to say hello day after day. At first Jackie only sneered, but little by little his warmth and openness began to penetrate her shell. One day she gambled on a nod, a day or so later mumbled, "Hi." She still thought he was just like the rest of the men she knew, even though his tactics might be a little subtler. But he was simply a nice guy whose heart had reached out with a gratuitous offering of sympathy and compassion. She couldn't believe he was honestly interested in her just for herself. But she began to hope it might be true.

A strange transformation began to take place. Her vulgar language was the first thing to change, followed by a new concern for personal appearance. It wasn't just the externals like combed hair, washed face, clean clothes: A new inner light started to show itself. As a person she was beginning to bloom, and his love seemed to be responsible for it all. He wasn't just playing social worker; he was deeply interested, he cared, he gave himself. In her response to his gift of friendship, she was called to an attitude of trust that became very painful. For she eventually found herself forced to turn away from all her old convictions and suspicions.

98

In a real sense, she died to her old self: the mask, the phony facade, the front she hid behind—all were shredded. At the end of that summer, he told her of his love and forced the issue. She was brought to a brink. If she acknowledged her love for him, she would be opening herself to the risk of rejection (and there had been plenty of that already); but after a torturous struggle, she made the leap and surrendered her heart in trust. It seemed she had abandoned everything, yet she felt richer for it. She had become a new person.

In a sense, this story of Jackie and Peter is the story of our personal relationship with Jesus Christ. The attraction is rooted in the beauty and enchantment, the personal magnetism and compelling power of the Master. His words are unlike any other's. . . .

"There is no greater love than this, that a man lay down his life for his friends. . . . I call you my friends. . . . Abide in my love. . . . These things I have spoken to you that my joy may be in you, and your joy may be filled. Peace is my gift to you. . . . Don't let your hearts be troubled. Trust in God and trust in me. . . . I'm going now to prepare a place for you, and after I have gone and prepared you a place, I'll return to take you with me, so that where I am you may be too." (Here I'm thinking of a deaf man named Charlie who at the moment of his death said, "For the first time, I hear someone coming.") Jesus says, "You didn't choose Me; no, I chose you." *These are phenomenal statements!* What deity of any great world religion has ever spoken with such breathtaking tenderness, incredible familiarity, indomitable confidence and spellbinding power!

We recognize that Jesus responds to needs and desires that we've long had, perhaps without being fully aware of them. He speaks to our innermost being, supplies our needs, satisfies our desires. In Him the obscure is illuminated, the uncertain yields to the certain, insecurity is replaced by a deep sense of security. In Him we find that we have come to understand many things that baffled us. The encounter with Jesus awakens us to possibilities we have never seen, and we know that this Person is what we have been seeking.

As with Jackie, this awareness is not without risk and anxiety. We know that we are now faced with a decision, brought to a brink, that evasion or postponement is a decision itself. We know that after this encounter our lives will never be the same again.

The Tremendous Lover, in the words of Francis Thompson, has pursued us relentlessly and declared Himself without reservation. "As the Father has loved Me, so I have loved you. Live on in My love."

To the extent that we have responded, to the extent that we have surrendered, made the leap and cried out, "I believe in the love of Jesus Christ for me," our lives are transformed. Like Jackie, we are different—our attitudes, thoughts, behavior. We live in a new relationship with Jesus, a situation of interpersonal communion, intimate friendship, authentic discipleship. As this love grows, our lives change dynamically. We are in the state of becoming "Christian" or what the apostle Paul describes as "maturing into the fullness of Christ."

Let's dig into the letters of Paul for a deeper understanding of this Christian maturity.

We have probably all encountered some difficulty in reading Paul. When he wrote a letter, it was not to talk about sports in Ephesus or the weather in Galatia. Paul was a passionate man who poured out the essence of his inner life. He was endowed with a fertile and active mind, both quick and penetrating. His mind raced ahead of his pen. His flow of language was so abundant that at times it approaches incoherence. He thought of a hundred things at once and used abrupt phrases, elliptical sentences, sudden unexpected digressions. But the incoherence is subordinated as Paul communicates his passionate conviction of the truth of the Gospel and his total personal dedication to Jesus.

Paul often repeats himself. One phrase—"in Christ"—occurs 164 times in the fourteen letters of Paul. Scripture scholars tell us that the whole Pauline canon could be reduced to these two words: "In Christ" is the key to Paul's thought, the summary of his teaching. Yet such a phrase—like "God bless," "Keep the faith," "Good luck," "How ya doin'?"—easily becomes a cliché, a trite expression devoid of any real meaning. Words, like anything else handled too often, soon depreciate in value. Just as a knife becomes blunted through constant use, words become dull through repetition, lose their edge, cease to bite into our minds.

For Paul, "in Christ" was far more than a conventional way of signing a letter. It was the meaning of time, the focal point of history: It contained the explanation of the universe. God made the world, Paul said, and all that is in it, for Christ. The Father loves the world only in Christ, and the world returns the Father's love only through Christ. He is the center of reality and the reason for its existence. Paul writes in Colossians 1:16, in Christ "all things were created: things in heaven and on earth . . . all things were created by him and for him."

If you ask yourself, "Why am I walking around this planet? Why do I exist?" Paul says, "You must answer: For the sake of Christ." If the angels were to ask, they must point to the Nazarene carpenter and make the same answer, "We exist for the sake of Christ." If the whole cosmos were suddenly to become articulate, then from north to south and east to west, it would cry out in chorus, "We exist for the sake of Christ." The name of Christ would issue from the seas and the deserts. It would be tapped out by the pattering rain. It would be written in the skies by the lightning. The storms would roar the name "Jesus Christ," and the mountains would echo it back. The sun's fierce nuclear furnace would blaze out: "The whole universe is full of Christ. He is the way, the truth, the life, the parable of the Father unraveling the riddle of existence."

This was Paul's christocentric concept of creation. The life of Christ was not a book in the library to be read but the air that he breathed, the medium in which he existed. He cries out in Philippians 1:21 (JB): "Life to me, of course, is Christ." In Galatians 2:20: "I no longer live, but Christ lives in me." In Romans 8:35: "Who shall separate us from the love of Christ? Shall trouble or hardship or persecution or famine or nakedness or danger or sword?" In Colossians 2:6: "Just as you received Christ Jesus as Lord, continue to live in him." In Him we live and move and have our being. Outside of Him there is no life. We go to God only in Christ, we are sons and daughters only in Christ, we inherit the Kingdom only in Christ, we live the life of God only in Christ.

What does this mean for our own maturing into the fullness of Christ? In 2 Corinthians 5:17, Paul says, "If anyone is in Christ, he is a new creation; the old has gone, the new has come!"

For Paul, a new creation meant a total renovation of the inner self, a change of mind and heart. It meant far more than the passive union achieved in water baptism. To be "in Christ," he told the Philippians, means to have in you the mind of Christ Jesus, to think as Christ thought, to have the ideals Christ had, to throb with the desires that filled Christ's heart, to replace all your natural actions to persons, events and circumstances with the response of Jesus Christ. In a word, a christocentric life means to live in the heart of Jesus, to share His tastes and aversions, to have the same interests, affections and attitudes, to be motivated in everything by His loving compassion. It means making the habitual

102

thought patterns of Jesus Christ so completely your own that truly "I no longer live, but Christ lives in me."

This was the triumph of the Spirit in a disciple named Francis from the village of Assisi. Romano Guardini once said that "Francis allowed Jesus Christ to become so transparent in his personality that his contemporaries called him 'the Christ of Umbria.'" Why are the personalities of so many pious and proper Christians so opaque? Why do we so seldom hear what the old lawyer said of John Vianney: "An extraordinary thing happened to me today: I saw Christ in a man!" Why doesn't the radiant loveliness of the Lord stream from our personalities? In the definition of Noah Webster, why aren't we "diaphanous or easily seen through"? Why aren't we windows into Jesus, working, laughing, crying, playing, loving? Why aren't we transparent disciples?

In varying degrees, of course, many Christians are. I think of the UPS driver who came to our door to tell my wife, Roslyn, and me about the drowning of his three-year-old son and to speak in tears of his love for Jesus and how he prays in his truck. I think of the dentist in St. Louis who treats everybody as better than himself and closer to the heart of Jesus; of the married couple on Long Island who laid bare their past sins and with stunning humility left Roslyn and me speechless as they bore witness to the merciful love of a redeeming God. And so without denying or minimizing the victories, great and small, of the Holy Spirit in our lives, let's explore further Paul's insight into maturing into the fullness of Christ.

In Romans 6:11 Paul says that through baptism we are united, made one with Christ. "Count yourselves dead to sin but alive to God *in Christ*" (italics added). By virtue of this union, all the actions of Jesus become ours as literally as if we had lived them ourselves. Through His passion, death and resurrection Christ won the power to share His own Spirit, to make our lives one with His.

All our actions—eating, drinking, sleeping, working—are thus potentially Christ's actions. But this potential must be actualized. Instead of a mindless drifting through the insignificant, apparently superficial and nonreligious events of the day, our passive union with Christ can be made active by creative acts of the will, intelligence and imagination. How?

By studying the life experiences of Jesus and relating them to our own; by poring over the Gospels and seeing the different scenarios not as historical events but as contemporaneous happenings reproducing themselves in our daily experience. Do we feel dry, weary, filled with a sense of failure? In the twinkle of an eye we can relate our mood to Jesus who one day felt the same way and collapsed exhausted by a well in Samaria. I can invite this tired Jesus into my very discouragement: "Jesus, here I am, whipped, wiped out, in the pits and all Yours."

Am I unjustly criticized, rejected, betrayed by a friend? I can touch the life of Jesus who faced the same things, and I can will to respond as He did. The power of His Spirit passes into my Spirit and the purpose of Pentecost is fulfilled—Christ is formed within me not just in peak moments of transcendental experience but in the nitty-gritty of daily life. I am confined to bed, sick, nauseous, racked with pain, utterly incapable of prayer. I have only to whisper, "It's Yours, my Friend," and it is no longer I who lie there, it is Jesus Christ. And so it goes. Jesus slept. I can unite my sleep with His. I'm having a rollicking good time at a Cajun barbecue in New Orleans. I shout with them, *"Laissez les bon temps rouler!"* Let the good times roll, and connect with Jesus who multiplied the wine at Cana to keep the party going (and gave His definitive answer to all the Puritans who frown on fun, detect demons at Disney World and scorn the celebration of secular humanism at the World's Fair).

By this continual shuttle action, I can bring Christ's experience into mine and unite mine with His. I am not speaking of a mechanical imitation of Jesus, for that is impossible. We live *in Christ* not by aping him but in the manner described in Philippians 2:5–7: "Your attitude should be the same as that of Christ Jesus: Who . . . made himself nothing, taking the very nature of a servant." Imitation could be a question of isolated actions; identification with Jesus touches the root of our actions, the principles by which we habitually judge and decide.

Remember the Gospel story of the woman with the hemorrhage. Touching only the hem of Christ's garment, she was healed. When Jesus asked, "Who touched Me?" Peter was astonished. "Who touched You? You're being jostled and hustled by the crowd on all sides!" But Jesus insisted, "I felt power go forth from Me." Among all those in physical contact with Jesus at that moment, this woman's touch was accompanied by faith—faith sufficient to unleash the divine power in the Master.

Far closer is our contact, we who have been made one with Jesus Christ through baptism. There we acquired the potential to participate in the "sacrament of the present moment"—to transform even our most mundane experiences into those of Christ. But we too must activate that contact through faith—strong faith that Jesus can come streaming into our lives and empower us to function and respond not from our ego-self but from our Spirit-self. But we must *will* the transformation. Only when we will to live *in Christ* do our actions become His. I am not speaking here of human willpower but of radical reliance on the Holy Spirit, who empowers us to transcend egoism, moodiness and laziness. I am speaking neither of the Pelagian mentality in which grace isn't necessary, nor of the Christian Charles Atlas nor of the Horatio Alger legend of the self-made saint. I am speaking with the same emphasis as the Trappist monk and psychoanalyst who when asked by a young Jewish convert, "How do I become a saint?" replied, *"Will it."*

The Spirit of Jesus enlightens our minds with wisdom and empowers our hearts with courage to choose to be one with Christ everywhere. Obviously we often fail. We have a tendency to enjoy things alone, to exclude Christ, to hug our little joys and sorrows to ourselves. But through daily prayer and discipline, we can mature into the fullness of Christ so that most of the tiny trivial problems of daily life lose their power to upset and unnerve us.

The personal transformation of the Christian is a mystery that cannot be pierced, but the effects of the transformation are set forth clearly in the New Testament—so clearly in fact that we try to obscure them. The bottom line is that the transparent Christian resembles Jesus, becomes a professional lover who is motivated by compassion in all that he or she thinks, says and does. In whatever language Paul describes this personal metamorphosis—putting on Christ, living in Christ, Christ living in the Christian or life in the Spirit—all point to a revolutionary change in our personal lives, our values, our habits, our attitudes. If we are true to this Christian love, it may kill us, impoverish us or disgrace us. In any event we are sure to lose at least some of the goods of this world, which Jesus took the trouble to point out are of no importance anyway.

This is what Paul means when he speaks 164 times of life *in Christ.* And our lives, yours and mine, can be played out on this high note of love, because lodged within us is the power, perhaps lying dormant, to make every thought, feeling, passion and emotion a full expression of our Spirit-self, of our life *in Christ.* Here in our hearts is the power to unify and make whole our total self, so that everything we have and are form but one personality—Jesus Christ living and loving in us.

Now someone may protest: "This is all very beautiful, but this isn't for me. This isn't for the ordinary person. This is to live like a saint." Paul's only reply is: "This is to live."

This is to live as fully a human being, moreover, because Jesus was fully human. To those who envisage life *in Christ* as sweetly insipid or airily otherworldly, the cleansing of the Temple, described in chapter 2 of John's Gospel, is a most disconcerting scene. It presents us with the inescapable portrait of an angry Savior. The magnanimous Jesus who said, "Forgive your neighbor seventy times seven," the meek Lamb of God who said, "Learn from Me for I am gentle and humble of heart," has fashioned a homemade whip and is tearing through the Temple overturning stalls and showcases, thrashing the merchants and roaring, "Get out of here! This isn't Winn Dixie! You will not turn sacred space into a supermarket!"

It would be an understatement to say that Jesus was upset. Blazing wrath, unmitigated rage are more accurate. Like fear, love and hatred, anger is an emotion both basic and necessary to human nature. When God drew aside the curtain of eternity and stepped into human history in the man Jesus, He fully assumed the human condition down to the last joyful or painful experience. The Word was made flesh; He was really one of us. Jesus is no stained glass figure, no pastel face on a religious card.

The Gospel portrait of Jesus is that of a man exquisitely attuned to His emotions and uninhibited in expressing them. In Luke's Gospel we see Him so offended by a discourtesy in the house of Simon the Pharisee that it provokes Him to say, "Simon, I came into your house and you didn't even say, 'Hi.'" In Mark He is so touched, so deeply moved by the tenderness of the woman who anoints His head with perfume, that He turns and says, "Write this down! Wherever the Good News is proclaimed, what she has done will be told also *in memory of her.*" (The next time you are with a male chauvinist, let your conversation be flavored with humor, as Paul says, and ask him where in the Gospel Jesus says, "Do this in memory of her." It's Mark 14:9. You may not blow him out of the water, but at least there'll be a leak in his boat.)

Scandalous as it may be, this is the Jesus of the Gospels: a man like us in all things but ungratefulness. A man consoled by the tears of a sinful woman, a man who experienced anger, irritation and fatigue. A man who drank His people's wine and sang their wedding songs. In so many ways and by so many signs did Jesus show us that He is fully human, that He has a sensitive human heart and longs to be treated as one who is human.

We don't hear much about the humanness of Jesus in certain Christian circles. Jesus said unto them: "Who do you say that I am?" And they replied, "You are the eschatological manifestation of the ground of our being, the Kerygma in which we find the ultimate meaning of our interpersonal relationships." Jesus said unto them: "What?"

The real danger today is that Jesus is transformed from a two-edged sword into a curiosity piece. The late Dorothy Sayers wrote:

> The people responsible for the crucifixion of Jesus never accused him of being a bore—on the contrary: they thought him too dynamic to be safe. It has been left for later generations to muffle up that shattering personality and surround him with a yawning ho-hum atmosphere of tedium. We have efficiently trimmed the claws of the Lion of Judah, certified him "meek and mild," and recommended him as a fitting household pet for pale curates and pious old ladies. To those who knew him, however, he in no way suggested a milk and water person; they objected to him as a dangerous firebrand. True, he was tender to the unfortunate, patient with honest inquiries, and humble before Heaven; but he insulted

respectable clergymen by calling them hypocrites . . . he went
to parties in disreputable company and was looked upon as a
drunkard and glutton . . . he assaulted indignant tradesmen
and threw them and their belongings out of the temple . . .
he showed no proper deference for wealth or social position
. . . and he asked disagreeably searching questions that could
not be answered by rule of thumb. He was emphatically not
a dull man in his human lifetime.[1]

God's self-disclosure in the man Jesus is mind-
boggling but not totally unforeseen. It is consistent
with the Old Testament and the fulfillment of Hebrew
prophecy.

In Isaiah 54, and later in Hosea 2, God pictures Himself as a husband and lover of His people. These images
provide a profound insight into Jewish religious experience, an insight that has led one modern Scripture
scholar to say that the fantastic humanness of the incarnation is really not so surprising in a religious tradition
of which Hosea was a part.

What God did through this prophet was to appropriate sexual imagery to Himself. Yahweh is as intimately
involved with Israel as a husband with his wife—and
no model wife, either. Israel was a harlot, unfaithful
to her husband, whoring around with false gods. But
Yahweh's passion for His bride was such that He simply
could not give her up. He desired her with a longing that
her infidelity couldn't cool. He permitted her to exercise
a power over Him that aroused His ardor even when
she had become a prostitute. As one Christian put it,
"Yahweh was hooked on His bride." He could not have
enough of her and His passion could not be dampened
by her many betrayals.

Sexual imagery is universal in human religious experience. But when the living God in whose presence Moses
had to remove his shoes is presented as a cuckolded hus-

band who relentlessly pursues His wayward wife, some Christians have protested that this is not only an outrageous symbol but a blasphemous one. Why? Because the prophet Hosea is implying that God doesn't just care for His people; Hosea implies that God is sexually aroused in the presence of His people. And that idea was shocking to the Jews, scandalous to their neighbors and remains an enormous stumbling block for the Jansenists and neo-Manicheans in our own day.

Are you aware that in the fourth century A.D., the Christian community borrowed and assimilated the spring fertility symbol of the Roman Empire and put it into our Easter liturgy? At the baptismal rite of the Easter vigil, a lighted candle is inserted into a vase of holy water to symbolize that when Jesus Christ rose from the dead He consummated His union with His bride the church.

It was certainly clear to fourth-century Christians that they were using a symbol of sexual intercourse in their Easter services. But while the practice has been continued down the centuries, its meaning has been carefully repressed. Generations of clergy have enacted the intercourse ritual and generations of laity have witnessed without comprehending the extraordinary notion it conveys. The symbolism speaks more forcefully than any sermon: Have you ignored the God of Abraham, Isaac and Jacob? Have you missed the message of the prophets? Do you find the New Testament too obtuse? Then let me ask you a question that you will surely understand:

Have you ever been sexually aroused to an intense degree? Really stimulated in a sensuous way? Passionately turned on? Both the Scripture and the liturgy of the Christian community say that human sexual arousal is but a pale imitation of God's passion for His people. That is why human love, though it is the best image we have, is still an inadequate image of God's love. Not because it overdoes it, but because human desire with all its emotion cannot compare with the passionate yearning of Jesus Christ. That is why saints can only stutter and stammer about the reality; why Blaise Pascal on his famous night of fire, November 21, 1654, could not speak a word; why Bede Griffiths wrote: "The love of Jesus Christ is not a mild benevolence: it is a consuming fire."

It is only the revelation that God is love that clarifies the happy irrationality of God's conduct and His relentless pursuit. For love tends to be irrational. It pursues in spite of infidelity. The Gospel account of the cleansing of the Temple tells us that sometimes love blossoms into jealousy and anger. Jesus' anger reveals His keen interest, His frantic involvement in His brothers and sisters coming into right relationship with Abba God.

Do you see why the Torah of the God of Hosts, why the Gospel of the Son of Man, is such a revolutionary revelation? What Christian in his or her right mind would dare to speak of God in such human, earthy terms unless God Himself had used them first? Our Western mentality is rather staid. Jews in their Semitic thought patterns are much more creative, poetic and imaginative than we literalistic Westerners. I think of a scene from the play *Gideon,* written by a Jew from Brooklyn named Paddy Chayefsky.

Gideon is out in the desert in his tent a thousand miles from nowhere, feeling deserted and rejected by God. One night God breaks into the tent and Gideon is seduced, ravished, overcome, burnt by the wild fire of God's love. He is up all night, pacing back and forth in his tent. Finally, dawn comes, and Gideon in his Brooklyn Jewish accent cries out, "God, O God, all night long I've thought of nuttin' but You, nuttin' but You. I'm caught up in the raptures of love. God, I want to take You into my tent, wrap You up, and keep You all to myself. God, hey God, tell me that You love me."

God answers: "I love you, Gideon."

"Yeah, tell me again, God."

"I love you, Gideon."

Gideon scratches his head. "I don't understand. Why? Why do You love me?"

And God scratches *His* head and answers, "I really don't know. Sometimes, My Gideon, passion is unreasonable."

This is the God of Jesus and the God revealed in Jesus. As theologian Bernard Bush writes,

> Not the normal God of religion who is said to love us but threatens us with punishment, but a God who cherishes and graces all people without qualification, a God whose whole and only desire is our happiness and fulfillment, a God who is grieved when we feel guilty about being happy and frightened that it won't last. Our God awareness is so flawed. Abba is hedged in by the God of "being on the safe side," the God of knock on wood, the capricious God of control who manipulates us into a state of free-floating anxiety and undefinable fear.

But Jesus says that if you will let the real God come into your life, then you will experience a huge freedom from the anxiety over survival; none of the usual concerns over livelihood will furrow your brow or weigh you down. You will experience a phenomenal freedom that makes it possible to forgive injuries, lend on demand, turn the other cheek, and look at an attractive person without lust. You won't hurry past the wino on the street and won't be afraid to dine with disreputable people. Open yourself to my God whose passionate love is unreasonable and trust Him wholeheartedly.

My brothers and sisters, Jesus is our God. He and the Father are one. He is the image of the invisible God. Our Jesus image makes all the difference. If we let the Lion of Judah run loose as Lord of our lives, He will not want us to be poor, broken or sad. Yet He may allow it, knowing that in these conditions we are more likely to let Him make us rich, whole and happy. If you let the real Jesus into your life, the God whose supreme desire is your happiness and fulfillment, you will want to throw out anything that is going to stop you from reaching His Kingdom. The brutal hyperboles about plucking out the eye, cutting off the hand or foot, become understandable in this context—and in no other. Jesus' teaching is full of wild exaggerations, for Jesus is a wild man. And He says to us, "It has pleased My Father to give you the Kingdom."

Our life in Christ. It's not an easy thing to grasp. Maybe you understand it only by living it. And maybe Augustine was right on the money when he wrote:

> Give me someone who loves, and he will understand what I am trying to say. Give me someone whose heart yearns, who feels the nostalgia of loneliness in this exile, who is athirst and sighs for a fatherland eternal, give me such a one and he will understand what I am trying to say. But if I must explain myself to ice-cold indifference, he will not understand.[2]

No one will have read so far in a book like this driven by ice-cold indifference, but by longing and desire for the Lord Jesus. My prayer for us all is that we may grasp more fully His love, which surpasses all knowledge—and that we mature into the fullness of Christ one day at a time.

FOR REFLECTION

Begin with five minutes of silent prayer, becoming aware in faith of God's indwelling presence and humbly asking the Spirit to speak to your heart through Scripture, personal reflection and the insights of others.

113

Let one of the group read aloud Galatians 2:19–20. Then focus on the following questions for personal reflection and group interaction.

1. Describe someone you know well whom you consider transparent. What are his or her qualities that you find so attractive?
2. Do you see yourself as transparent? Illustrate by examples.
3. Ask others in the group what they most like about you.

CHAPTER 7

Living Out of the Center

Skeptic that I am over the unholy alliance of religion and politics, and personally uneasy around Christian things that glitter, I went to Washington with low expectations. Was Jesus Christ going to be used for personal gain and political advantage? Were we going to pay lip service to His Lordship, wave Christian banners and dance our way around the demands of discipleship, while garnering free publicity as "good religious folks"?

I can really relate to the temptation of the contemporary world to look good but not be good. When I was a closet alcoholic, I almost always drank myself into oblivion out of the public eye. Through an elaborate series of pretenses and disguises (you know, Listerine for tell-tale breath and Visine for bloodshot eyes), I tried to cover up my impoverished inner self. When I glanced into a store window, it was to check out myself more than the merchandise on display. Even sober, I still sneak glances at myself to make sure that I don't lose my trial membership in the fellowship of "beautiful people." I am painfully aware of these small vanities in myself. I hear the Southern novelist Walker Percy when he asks: "Why is it that, when you are shown a group photograph in which you are present, you always (and probably covertly) seek yourself out? Is it to see what you look like? Don't you know what you look like?"

Concern for appearance might be the American original sin; it goes right along with fake furs, paste jewelry, sawdust hot dogs and deceptive advertising. Such self-deception is subtle, even for a while relatively harmless. But the temptation to settle for looking good while everything is falling apart inside can be dangerous. After a long season of accepting appearances for reality, a Christian forgets what truth even sounds like. We end up asking with Pontius Pilate, "What is truth?" The prayer of Gregory Nazianzen, *esse quam videri*—"to be rather than to appear to be"—rises often from my heart. Perhaps this largely explains my skepticism about the electronic church, media evangelism and presidential prayer breakfasts. My distrust is rooted in my own preoccupation with appearances and the false face I see in the store window.

The prayer breakfast opened with Senator Lawton Chiles of Florida announcing matter-of-factly that television cameras and the press were not permitted at the breakfast. So much for the publicity theory. Billy Graham prayed for world peace and for President Reagan who, he said, had been a pastor to the American people during the shuttle *Challenger* tragedy. Next, Bill Ashton, a member of the Capitol Hill Police who prays with six U.S. senators each Thursday morning, gave a powerful and passionate testimony to his personal relationship with Jesus. He was followed by Mary Beth Kissee, who with a voice like Birgit Nilsson's sang "We Shall Behold Him." Like vapor rising from the ground, a sense of God's presence filled the room. Then the president, who was celebrating his seventy-fifth birthday, spoke without a script of his personal relationship with Christ. Later, Senator William Armstrong of Colorado commented, "In all the years I've known Ronald Reagan, I have never heard him talk the way he did or in the tone of voice he did this morning." Reagan spoke about Mother Teresa, his personal relationship with her and how her faith sustains her in eighteen-hour days of ministry to the poor. The president observed that when a tree is cut down, a sprout often rises from the stump, a sprout of hope.

Referring to his own life, he said, "I'm sure that you have found, as I have, that when we are cut down by adversity and suffering, a hope springs forth borne of our trust in God." In the next two minutes President Reagan said four times, "Joy is God's gift to us—a joy that is not superficial but a joy born of sorrow and tragedy that one day we shall enjoy eternal peace with Him."

Following the president's remarks, Wintley Phipps, a tenor from Texas, sang, "He Is Coming." I looked around at the 3,500 guests in the banquet room of the Washington Hilton. Most people's eyes were closed in prayer. The focus was no longer on the dais—President Reagan and Nancy, Vice President Bush and Barbara, Treasury Secretary Jim Baker and Susan, John Stennis, Arthur Burns, Billy Graham—but on Jesus Christ who had called us all together. As Phipps' voice soared an octave, "Oh, He's comin'," people turned toward the door as if expecting the arrival of the risen Lord. It was a profound experience. The prayer breakfast had become a prayer meeting where Jesus was exalted as Lord of history. I walked out the door humbled and grateful to reflect that

117

the incense of prayer and praise rises each week from Capitol Hill where forty members from the House and six from the Senate gather in regular fellowship. What if this really *were* the pattern of our national priorities? What if Jesus *were* the focus, corporately and individually? If we call ourselves Christians, in fact, wouldn't this have to be the case?

Christians, *if* they are more than nominally so, accept the supreme, even unique importance of Jesus for the meaning of human life, both the life of the race and the life of the individual person. To borrow a well-worn phrase, they believe that Jesus is not only the most important thing, He is the only thing. They believe that without Him nothing in human life and human affairs has any significance; without Him there are no values that are not transitory. For them the standard chronology of B.C., "Before Christ," and A.D., "Anno Domini"—the year of the Lord—expresses a truth: The life of Jesus is the central event in human history according to which that entire history must be evaluated and judged.

The truth of Christianity is not a doctrine but a person. It is the reality of Jesus Christ that is the foundation stone of all Christian hope. Romano Guardini has some burning phrases on the centrality of Jesus for Christian life, belief and behavior.

> What is certain in life and death—so certain that everything else may be anchored in it? The answer is: the love of Christ . . . only Christ's love is certain. We cannot even say God's love; for that God loves us we know ultimately only through Christ. And even if we did know without Christ that God loved us, love can be inexorable, and the more noble it is, the more demanding. Only through Christ do we know that God's love is forgiving. . . . What has been said so often and so inadequately is true: the heart of Jesus Christ is the beginning and end of all things.[1]

118

Jesus is not only the founder of Christianity but its content. He is central to Christianity in a way that no other founder of a religion has dared to claim for himself.

Every religion has three elements, the intellectual element, the ritual or sacramental element and the personal or mystical element. The intellectual element comprises what a religion believes, its doctrines or dogmas. The ritual element consists in the sacrifices and ceremonies of worship, and the mystical element is the personal relationship with the God we adore. In Christianity Jesus stands at the center of each of these aspects. He is the intellectual element, for He is the doctrine we believe. He *is* the Revelation. He is also the ritual element. When the Christian community gathers for the communal meal, Jesus *is* the Eucharist. The other sacraments are His gestures prolonged in time and space. As St. Augustine said: "It is Christ alone who baptizes, confirms, forgives, and heals." And Jesus is the center of the mystical life. In Him we live and move and have our being. Outside of Jesus there is no personal communion with God, no mystical life. We are sons and daughters of Abba only in Christ Jesus; we inherit the Kingdom only in Christ Jesus. Christian mysticism is essentially a personal relationship in which one member is a human being and the other is the eternal God revealed in Jesus.

> Jesus . . . is the center of Christianity not only because He is the center of the intellectual, ritual, and mystical elements but further because He is the center of God's original revelation in the Old Testament. . . . Adam, the first man, prefigures the Christ, the firstborn of many brothers and sisters who will be born again to the life of the Spirit. Moses, the great Lawgiver of the Old Testament, recalls to us the Christ who will set His people free from the Law with its heavy and intolerable burdens and who brings the new law of love. . . . Joshua, the Liberator, points to Jesus who bought the church in His Blood,

119

freeing us from the dominion of sin. . . . The entire Old
Testament finds its fulfillment only in the unique event
when God Himself assumed our human nature.[2]

In the New Testament, Jesus upstages everyone else.
He is not only the center of the Gospel; He is the whole
Gospel. He is the Good News. The four evangelists never
focus on another personality. Fringe people stay on the
fringe, marginal men and women stay on the margin. No
one else is allowed to take center stage. Various individu-
als are introduced only to interrogate, respond or react to
Jesus. Nicodemus, the Samaritan woman, Peter, Thomas,
Mary Magdalene, Caiaphas, Pilate and all the others form
the backdrop to the person of Jesus. He dwarfs everyone
else. This is as it should be, for the New Testament is
kairos—the hour of salvation—and Jesus is that salvation. When the final curtain falls, He will upstage all the
Caesars and Napoleons, popes, presidents, Ph.D.s and
pundits, all the famous and powerful people who have
ever lived in the course of human history. Every man and
woman who has ever drawn breath will be appraised,
evaluated and measured solely in terms of his or her
personal relationship with the Carpenter from Nazareth.
As the late T. S. Eliot put it, "O my soul, be prepared to
meet Him who knows how to ask questions." This is the
proper theological understanding of the New Testament
and the eschatological Lordship of Jesus Christ.

"What think you of Christ, whose son is He?" is the
crucial question of the Gospel. To provide the answer is
the purpose of the New Testament: "That you may know
God and the One He has sent, Jesus Christ."

Jesus demanded faith in Himself. He reproached the
disciples in the storm-tossed boat, "O you of little faith."
And He demanded hope in Himself: "Come to Me, all
you who labor and find life wearisome, and I will refresh
you." And in emphatic terms, He demanded love of Him-

self: "He who loves his mother or father more than Me is not worthy of Me."

In a word, Jesus Christ has made Himself the vital center of the Christian life. Jesus is not only the heart of Christianity, He is the center of humanity and reveals to us what it means to be human. To be a Christian is to be fully human. Do we Christians really believe that? What does it mean to be fully human, living a life of which Jesus is the center? What does it mean to live out of the center?

First, it means that an authentic Christian is quite literally *ec-centric*—that is, off center, so far as managing, directing and controlling one's own life is concerned. This demands a revolutionary shift away from focus on self. In the sixteenth century Nicolaus Copernicus and Galileo Galilei demonstrated that the sun, not the earth, is the center of the solar system. The Copernican revolution was just that. It shook the very foundations of astronomy and science. These two men called for a radical rethinking and readjustment of the way we envisioned the cosmos—so radical that Galileo was condemned as a heretic and excommunicated from the church. Do we see what a revolutionary reorientation Jesus brought, what a radical readjustment Jesus called for when He said we are not the center of our own lives?[3]

In our present generation when there is so much talk of self-fulfillment, self-determination, self-decision, self-confidence, self-respect, the apostle Paul seems at the very least *ec-centric* when he says, "I live now not with my own life but with the life of Christ who lives in me." Living out of the center effects a profound transformation within us. Things that once seemed so important become peripheral. As a teenager I wanted to be a professional golfer. For ten years I played forty-five holes a day and caddied to buy new clubs, tees and balls. I worked, slept, dreamed and played golf unceasingly. Then in February

1956, in the seminary, I met Jesus. Every Saturday was a free day, and seminarians were allowed to play golf for free on a nearby course. Instead, I found myself jogging three miles through the woods to a Carmelite chapel to spend the day alone with the Lord. I didn't give up golf entirely. It just didn't seem that important anymore.

Paul's fascination with Jesus and determination to make Him the center of his life brought him to say, "I believe that nothing can happen that will outweigh the supreme advantage of knowing Christ Jesus. For Him I have accepted the loss of everything, and I look on everything as so much rubbish if only I can have Christ and be given a place in Him."

Living out of the center means sharing Jesus' intimate experience of God as Father. The meaning of the word *father* in the Scriptures has two aspects: First of all, it means lord and ruler, full control and authority. Jesus acknowledged the absolute sovereignty of His Father. He never attempted to justify God for all the muddle, pain and tragedy in the world. In Luke 13, when people tell Jesus about some Galileans murdered by Pilate, He does not defend God or justify His reasons for allowing people to suffer. Indeed, He reminds them about the eighteen on whom the tower of Siloam fell. Jesus makes no effort to exonerate God from the scandal of suffering, to bail Him out, to rationalize or minimize the presence of tragedy in His world. He surrenders without reservation to the infinite wisdom and awesome majesty of God.

The Christian living out of the center stares long and compassionately at the skeletal bodies of Ethiopian children, the demented locked up in insane asylums, the addicts on Skid Row, the children with Down's syndrome, and attempts neither to justify God's silence nor to get Him off the hook by lamely explaining why bad things happen to good people, or pointing to the randomness of the universe, or anything else. The God of Jesus Christ is God, Lord and Ruler, and the Christian surrenders with boundless confidence because God is also Father. Don't try to understand it. You won't succeed. Don't try to see it. You can't. Try to live it, and you will be living out of the center.

The second aspect of the word *father* in Scripture involves care, concern, compassion and reliability. We are not only invited but actually called to enter into this warm, liberating experience of fatherhood. In Romans Paul is explicit: "Those who are led by the Spirit of God are sons of God. For you did not receive a spirit that makes you a slave again to fear, but you received the Spirit of sonship. And by him we cry, '*Abba*, Father'" (Romans 8:14–15).

> Fear both of the past and the future, cripples us. On one hand, it can make us defensive, closed to any progress, and on the other it can make us rush forward for fear of not being "with it." Fear can cause unkindness to others and phariseeism with God. All we do under the impulse of fear does not bear the fruits of the Spirit. The deep-rooted realization that God is our Abba drives out fear. A new freedom blossoms, the same freedom that made Jesus so attractive and authentic.[4]

In my final year at the seminary, I developed a bad case of hay fever. Every morning at 5:30, just as the cleric master began to lead sixty seminarians in prayer, I would have an attack of coughing and sneezing. One day he called me into his office and accused me of insubordination, claiming that I was deliberately disrupting morning prayer with my antics. He warned me that my future actions would be monitored and that my ordination to the priesthood, just four months away, was in jeopardy. It was a devastating moment. I left his office angry and frightened, filled with self-pity and confusion. I stumbled to the chapel, sank to my knees and began to silently whisper the name *Jesus* over and over. Then something wondrous happened. In a moment of truth and breathtaking freedom, I realized that ordination to the priesthood was not so almighty important. It pleased Jesus more to have me be my real self—hay fever allergies and all—than a cowed and intimidated priest. I left the chapel and never once looked over my shoulder. I was ordained the following May still sneezing.

In the history of Christian discipleship, this little incident scarcely ranks alongside the heroism of the martyrs and saints. Still, it gave me a taste of living out of the center and experiencing the freedom of the children of God.

Living out of the center frees us from the tyranny of peer pressure. Living to please the Father, as Jesus did, becomes the basic impulse of a Christian's life—more important than pleasing people. And this requires a remarkable degree of freedom. Jesus was not intimidated by public opinion, by what "others will think." In order to be free for the outcasts, the sinners, the marginals in His social world, Jesus had to keep His distance from the expectations and the moralizing judgments of the authorities and the respectable. When he walked with the notorious sinner Zacchaeus through the streets of Jericho, He was not fazed by the scandalized murmurs of the crowd. He wasn't looking around anxiously, fearing what people might say. He was neither afraid of their rejection nor concerned about stepping on toes. He was going to the home of Zacchaeus because this sinner was a child of His Father, that was all. And that's the name of that tune.

"There is a kind of tyranny of public opinion which we often find at work in our lives. What will the neighbors think? . . . The expectations of others often act as a subtle but controlling pressure on our behavior."[5] The crowd does not take kindly to nonconformity. It is the scorn of our peers probably more than anything else that hinders our living out of the center. The fear of ridicule paralyzes us more effectively than flat-out opposition. How much good is left undone because of this fear! The irony is that the opinions we fear most are not those of people we really respect, yet these very persons influence our lives more than we want to admit. This desire to stand well with "them" can lead to an appalling mediocrity and a frightening unfreedom.

Living out of the center shapes and forms a liberated Christian. Albert Camus once said, "The only way to deal with an unfree world is to become so absolutely free that your very act of existence becomes an act of rebellion." There is nothing more maddening to the mob than a free person.

One night at Coney Island a group of us were standing outdoors at Nathan's munching hot dogs. A few yards away in the center of the boardwalk, a man was pouring a can of beer on the head and down the blouse of a pregnant girl of maybe fifteen. He was describing aloud in lurid detail how he had sexually abused her and what he had in mind later. She appeared slightly intoxicated; at any rate she was crying. "What a zoo!" one of our group said. "Let's split."

We started toward the car when, like a bell sounding deep in my soul, I heard, *Who are you?*

I stopped as if my shoes were stuck to the pavement. "I am a son of my Father," I said.

That girl is My daughter.

I went back, drew the girl aside and spoke with her for several minutes. Some bystanders began to taunt: "Pimp! Whoremonger!" That night I wept, not for them but for myself, for the countless times I have played the silent sentinel, afraid to acknowledge the presence of the Son of Man in the least of my brothers and sisters. How often I've seen human dignity being degraded and been content to moralize about the situation and walk away. James writes in his letter: "When a man knows the right thing to do and does not do it, he sins."

On a recent flight to South Carolina from New Orleans, I had the opportunity for a lengthy period of centering prayer. I closed my eyes, silently began to repeat the name of Jesus and became conscious in faith of Jesus in my heart. During a two-hour layover in the Atlanta airport, I decided I had better get a shoeshine to look more presentable to the Episcopalians to whom I would be speaking. An elderly man shined my shoes for the going rate of one dollar and fifty cents. I handed him two dollars and said, "Now you get up in the chair and I'll shine your shoes."

He said, "Huh? What?"

"I won't charge you."

He stared at me suspiciously. "What for, then?"

"Because you're my brother."

He really looked disconcerted then. Finally, he said, "Well, when I ain't busy the boss leaves me some shoes to shine. But thank you anyway."

When I saw tears in his eyes, I reached out and hugged him, and he said softly, "No white man ever talked to me like that before."

These two incidents stand out in my memory not because they are typical but because they are so very rare in my experience. Most of the time I'm living on the surface rather than out of the center, either lost in mindless daydreaming or caught up in my own little universe of plans and projects.

What these occasional breakthroughs into centered living do is to help me see that sin and grace can be present at the same time in the same person. Remember that scene in Matthew 16 where Peter has just received an inspiration from the Father about the real identity of Jesus and is affirmed by his Master. The very next minute Peter is listening to another voice, which brings the rebuke: "Get behind Me, Satan; these are the standards of men, not of God." Paul agonizes over the same thing in Romans 7:18–19, 24–25: "I have the desire to do what is good, but I cannot carry it out. For what I do is not the good I want to do; no, the evil I do not want to do—this I keep on doing. . . . What a wretched man I am! Who will rescue me from this body of death? Thanks be to God—through Jesus Christ our Lord! So then, I myself in my mind am a slave to God's law, but in the sinful nature a slave to the law of sin."

It has never been expressed so eloquently, so succinctly and so forcefully: Paul can even find the hand of God and summon a response of praise in contemplating his own sinfulness!

Living out of the center makes a difference in so many ways. It enables us to see that the church is a place in which to celebrate and not always reform, that the world is a place that should be enjoyed, not always acted upon, that life is an experience without an agenda, that love, the greatest of all our doings, is always unearned, undeserved and unexpected.

Living out of the center enables me to speak and act from greater strength, to heal and forgive rather than hold grudges, to be capable of greatness of heart when confronted with pettiness, to discover that the only valid reason for doing the right thing is because it *is* the right thing. When Daniel Berrigan lectured at Loyola University here in New Orleans a couple of years ago, someone in the audience asked him, "Dan, why do you keep knocking yourself out for the peace movement? You've paid your dues. You've lost your reputation in many dioceses as a sound theologian, you've spent five years in the slammer for pouring blood on draft files in Maryland, your friends have scattered, your honor is questioned and your health has deteriorated. Can you see any real change in the posture of the American government or in the hearts of people?"

Berrigan paused, reflected for a full minute and replied in a forceful double negative, "I cannot *not* do what I am doing. I do it because it is the right thing to, not for any changes it might accomplish."

There is a profound truth here. If we are motivated to give prophetic witness, stage a demonstration or embark on a crusade simply to see immediate visible results, tangible fruits, and these changes are not quickly forthcoming, we can easily become cynical, disillusioned and disenchanted. An example from recent American history: The hippies of the sixties have become the yuppies of the eighties.

A group of radical evangelicals called the Sojourners held a national conference in Washington, D.C., called "Peace Pentecost 1985." Peacefully demonstrating at six key locations in the city, they protested against things like the Afghanistan invasion, South African apartheid, the death penalty, the United States' Central American policy, inadequate assistance to poor women. What the Reverend Jim Wallis, leader of the Sojourners and a gentle man who lives out of the center, said of the effort applies to all Christian endeavor: "The difference that we make will be determined in the end simply by how faithful we are to the Gospel. The rest has to be left to God."

Living out of the center enables us to blend for a moment into a greater background than our own fears, to merely be still and to know that God is God. It means that I don't figure out, I don't analyze. I simply lose myself in the experience of just being alive, of being in a community of believers, simply knowing that it's good to be there, even if I don't know where "there" is or why it's good. An inner stillness assures me that it is enough right now to be centered, to be in Christ Jesus, and that gratefulness is both the heart of living and the heart of prayer.

In my days of wine and roses, sour wine and withered roses, when I was stashing vodka bottles in the bathroom, the glove compartment and the geranium pot, I saw my life as a complete waste—not only for the things I was doing but for the things I wasn't doing, the meager, paltry, stingy response I was making to Christ in the least of my brothers. It was a long winter of discontent, guilt, fear, shame and unbearable hypocrisy. The future held out only the bleak prospect of a wet brain and an alcoholic shuffle, commitment to the funny farm or premature death. The disease meant failure with no redeeming aspect whatsoever.

But living out of the center has taught me that every failure *succeeds in some way.* It provides the opportunity not only to humble the self but also to be gentle with the failure of others. If your life or mine was an untarnished success story, an unbroken upward spiral toward holiness, we might never come to understand the human heart.

Living out of the center is not a rarefied, spaced-out state. It has helped me achieve connections and insight into the Word of God that were hitherto hidden. For example, Jesus told us to consider ourselves the least of all. He also told us that what we do for the least brother we do to Him. Since whatever is done for the least is done for the Lord, our compassion must start with ourselves. Before I am asked to show compassion toward my brothers and sisters in their suffering, I am asked to accept the compassion of Jesus in my own life, to be transformed by it and to become caring and compassionate toward myself in my own failure and hurt, in my own suffering and need. His love is not conditioned by what we are or do. He will be gracious and compassionate toward us no matter what our track record, for that is what "Jesus" means—the One who saves. Those who live out of the center know in their bones that they are poor and sinful, but there is a spirit of self-acceptance without self-concern. This is the heart of the Gospel —that we can be gracious and compassionate toward ourselves.

My brother or sister, if you live out of the center, you win. On a given day you might be more depressed than anything else, but when your life is hidden with Christ in God, you win. The roof might collapse, the empire may crumble, you may be transferred to Pago-Pago, but with Christ in you, your hope of glory, you win. You might be thinking low thoughts in high places—sitting in church wondering about the preacher's hairstyle, or what you would say if the president gave you a phone call, or what other name you might have chosen for yourself, or could you witness to Christ if you were being tortured with electric shock or with a little body work could you look like Rambo.

But if you live out of the center on and off during the day, you win. In our kitchen we have a saying enclosed in an old beaten-up wooden frame: "God will not look you over for medals, diplomas, or honors, but for scars." In the middle of Lent all you may have are your wounds and your last shred of hope. But with the risen victorious Jesus at the center of your life, you win. That was all the early Christian community had against Jerusalem, Rome and Athens, and the Christians won. That's no rhetoric; that's history. They had only Jesus, yet we keep thinking that we need something else.

FOR REFLECTION

Begin with five minutes of silent prayer, becoming aware in faith of God's indwelling presence and humbly asking the Spirit to speak to your heart through Scripture, personal reflection and the insights of others.

Let one of the group read aloud John 15:1–5. Then focus on the following questions for personal reflection and group interaction.

1. What degree of freedom have you attained from peer pressure and the expectations of others? Cite an example.
2. Share your experience of a time when a personal failure became a blessing.
3. Living out of the center calls us to be alert and attentive to the whisperings of the Spirit throughout the day. Classics like Brother Lawrence's *The Practice of the Presence of God,* Thomas Keating's *Open Mind, Open Heart* and Richard Foster's *Prayer* have proved of inestimable help for countless disciples. Share what has helped you to remain aware of God's presence when the inevitable distractions of daily living pull you away. When you go to a movie, does Jesus stand outside on the sidewalk? When you step into a sailboat, does God stay ashore?

CHAPTER 8

Reckless Confidence

hristian commitment does not require unbridled emotion. Jesus is not asking for weeping and wailing or balloons and guitars. All He asks is that we live our Christian commitment with confidence, that we act out in trust day by day the dying-rising that Holy Week commemorates. Are you dying daily to self? Theologian Walter Burkhart writes:

To die to self is to live to others and to God. In my experience that sort of daily dying makes two requirements on you. One, you come to your brothers and sisters accepting your own brokenness. Not fearless and tearless, not unscarred and unshaken. Quite the contrary: you are a wounded healer, dreadfully vulnerable. In giving life to others, you die a little each time, each day. Two, you have to destroy the smallness in you, the narrowness that plagues human living—where you are all wrapped up in yourself, where all that matters is what you want and what you need, your own little hurts and secret joys. No!

The drama of Holy Week cries *No*. If you are risen with Christ, then for the love of Christ, live a risen life! Think big and love lots. Against all the odds, you will even feel better.

I want to make a bold, unqualified and unequivocal statement: The key events of the Lent-Easter cycle—the death of Jesus Christ on the cross on Good Friday and His glorious breakthrough to new life on Easter morning—are not merely a summoning but an empowering to a life of *reckless confidence* regarding our past, our present and our future. It is confidence and nothing but confidence, immense, unshakable, reckless, raging confidence that leads to love, to life, to freedom, to Jesus.

The great German theologian Karl Rahner writes in his book *Foundations:* "A person is always a Christian in order to become one, and this is also true of what we are calling a personal relationship to Jesus Christ in faith, confidence and love." A new possibility exists. We can be more than we are at any one moment.

In Mark 11:22–24 Jesus says, "Have faith in God. . . . I tell you the truth, if anyone says to this mountain, 'Go, throw yourself into the sea,' and does not doubt in his heart but believes that what he says will happen, it will be done for him. Therefore I tell you, whatever you ask for in prayer, believe that you have received it, and it will be yours."

Do you see how far Jesus calls us to push our confidence? Believe that you have it already!

It is the charism of saints, who are enlightened and inspired by the Holy Spirit, to trust radically. Paul pours out his whole heart in Philippians 4:13 in the cry, "I can do everything through him who gives me strength." That is raging confidence.

When Jesus says in John 16, "Have confidence in Me, be brave, cheer up," He is calling us to unconditional abandonment to God's mercy over the sins of our past, unwavering confidence that they have been not only forgiven but entirely forgotten.

A recovering alcoholic asked to take his fifth step with me. The fifth step of the AA program reads: "Acknowledge to God, another human being and myself the exact nature of my wrongs." In traditional language, it was a general confession. Though a priest for twenty-one years, I heard this man confess sins committed under the influence of alcohol, drugs and witchcraft that I'd not only never read about in texts on moral theology but never heard before. It was a sordid story of debauchery and shame. All the pent-up guilt, fear and self-hatred accumulated during years of degradation cascaded forth in a torrent of tears. Above the din of his convulsive crying, I spoke to this man of the compassion of Jesus, of the Father's unbearable forgiveness, infinite patience and tender love, of the finding of the lost sheep, the joy in heaven over the return of one sinner. As I spoke, the most amazing thing happened. The flow of tears stopped; the man's face became transfigured. His mouth was wide open in wonder, his eyes transfixed in rapture. The Word of God pierced his heart; the truth set him free. He was an awestruck witness to reckless confidence without limit in God's mercy.

Some people play with Gospel imagery, mesmerize you with word games. They believe what they are saying and persuade others to belief. But the ideas stay lodged in their intellect and the words stay caught in their throats. Beautiful head trips are all they are. They never internalize mercy. They never risk, they never leap in trust, they never surrender to reckless confidence. The worst sin in their lives is that they exempt themselves from grace.

A classic example is Father Hugh Donlon in Andrew Greeley's novel *Ascent into Hell.* Father Donlon dazzles

135

the congregation with spellbinding oratory. "We must remember," he proclaims, "that we do not earn God's forgiveness by our sorrow or by our reparation. God's love is a given. It is always there, waiting patiently for us. We need only turn to Him to receive it. He is pleased with our efforts but even more pleased with us. That's why He made us. You cannot earn God's love, because He gave it to you before you started to earn it."

This little sermon is a beautiful distillation of the Gospel. But while Father Donlon preaches a God of mercy to others, it is a God of justice who dominates his own personal life. Only shipwreck and heartbreak finally force him to turn his own words on himself.

Again it is the saints, those extravagant lovers of God and people, who challenge us to push our confidence to extreme limits. Paul writes in 1 Timothy 1:14–15: "The grace of our Lord was poured out on me abundantly, along with the faith and love that are in Christ Jesus. Here is a trustworthy saying that deserves full acceptance: Christ Jesus came into the world to save sinners—of whom I am the worst."

Saints of modern times say things like this: "The good Lord is more eager to pardon a repentant sinner than a mother to rescue her child from a fire."

And: "Our sins are grains of sand beside the great mountain of the mercies of God." Grains of sand! Another saint says: "The moment we ask forgiveness, God throws our sins over His shoulder. He forgets them, He annihilates them; they shall never reappear."

The alcoholic whose fifth step I heard showed me the next day what he had written afterward on a piece of paper: "Dear Jesus, in thanksgiving for what You have done for me, I will make known to my brothers and sisters how kind You are toward sinners, and that Your mercy prevails over all malice, that nothing can destroy it, that no matter how many times, or how shamefully we fall, or how criminally, a sinner need not be driven to despair of Your pardon. It is in vain that Your enemy and mine sets new traps for me every day. He will make me lose everything else before the confidence that I have in Your mercy."

My friends, one thing that I have learned over the past twenty-eight years is this: the Jesus of my journey will never say to me, "Brennan, you were too reckless, you confided in Me too much, you trusted beyond reasonable limits, you hoped too much of Me. You should have only played with My word, 'Have confidence in Me,' rather than foolishly acting it out." No—the Christ of my life would never say that. You see, the litany of His saving acts of lovingkindness in my life gives firm support to reckless confidence. My history, like the history of the Israel of God, is a celebration of His faithfulness.

He called me out of marriage at the age of twenty-two when I wasn't ready for it, and twenty-five years later called me into it when I was. At the age of twenty-three, on the very day when I was preparing to leave the seminary in frustration, He baptized me in His Holy Spirit: February 8, 1956. And in April 1975, when I was lying in the gutter in Fort Lauderdale, Florida, barefoot, in an alcoholic fog, and my worst fear was that I might give up inside, He delivered me from fear and rescued me from myself.

The next time you are tempted to doubt God's faithfulness, write your own psalm of thanksgiving, remembering when He rescued you from darkness and turned your darkness into light. (And when you have a misunderstanding with your spouse or best friend, and unkind words are exchanged, and a quarrel ensues, remember when she or he in unfeigned love reached out to you. What you heard was probably not what the other meant and what you said was not what he or she heard.)

There is a beautiful echo of reckless confidence in Paul's advice to Timothy: "I urge, then, first of all, that requests, prayers, intercession and thanksgiving be made for everyone" (1 Timothy 2:1). Again from the writer of Hebrews in chapter 11, verse 1: "Faith is being sure of what we hope for and certain of what we do not see."

One of the most rattling witnesses to raging confidence is the Good Thief. Christian tradition has named him Dismas, and the story goes that he was a terrorist, a womanizer and a boozer. Yet, in a gesture of chutzpah so incredible that it would make any pickpocket or second-story man blush, he cried out, "Lord, remember me when You come into Your kingdom." And Jesus replied, "This day you will be with Me in paradise." One outrageous overture of reckless confidence wiped away a lifetime of sin. Dismas was given heaven in a moment.

As we stand on Calvary on Good Friday, one truth we learn is not to apply to the heart of Jesus the measure of our own stingy little hearts, so mean, so narrow and so hard. If we make Him as fussy, unforgiving and vindictive as we are at our worst, we will never comprehend how good, how patient and compassionate, how gentle and extravagant Jesus of Nazareth really is.

Jesus said, "He who sees Me sees the Father." From our brother Jesus, who alone knows the Father, we learn that there is welcoming love, unconditional acceptance, a relentless and eternal affection that so far exceeds our human experience that even the passion and death of Jesus are only a *hint* of it. Think on that for a moment: the torn, broken, lacerated, spit-covered, blood-drenched body of Jesus is only a hint of the Father's love. The very substance of our faith is the unwavering confidence that beyond this hint lies love beyond measure.

Oh, how I pray that everybody would understand what I feel. Where have all the prophets gone?

One of the telltale signs in the contemporary American church that trust in God is on the wane is the meteoric rise of legalistic religion. It will continue to flourish and attract an enormous number of devotees. For legalism is born of fear. It is a religious response to human fear. What makes legalism so attractive is that it meets a basic human need—security.

It makes absolute something that is humanly manufactured—man-made laws—and then goes on to justify its position by declaring that what has been absolutized is so by God's will. As Dick Westley notes in his book *Redemptive Intimacy,* the advantages of that reasoning are not small. We create a very solid foundation for our lives, because the God who has been absolutized by us *can never surprise us,* since He is in a way a being of our own making. We know what we have put into Him, and so we know exactly what we can expect to get out of Him. We planned it that way. Keep the laws and the laws will keep you. And so we invest our lives with conviction and certainty, not to say fanaticism, which are the hallmarks of nearly every legalist.

The risk of living in union with Jesus and hearing His voice *in our own lives* is too scary, so let's decide that the voice will sound only in the Bible, the official pronouncements of the church and our security network of human-made moral standards. It's an effective way of coping with God, reducing Him to human size and guaranteeing that we will not have to make way for the unsettling and new in our hearts. Legalists develop a false sense of security by the observance of church laws. As Scripture scholar John McKenzie writes: "Morality spoils their religion. They suffer from a legalistic hangup. They believe that fulfilling the external prescriptions of the law automatically guarantees the fulfillment of the purpose of the law. But if the fact of my adhering to laws (which I may truly need) does not further the final goal of my life, which is to know Christ Jesus and live his Gospel, then mere external conformity does little if anything."

The sixteenth-century mystic Ignatius of Loyola said of himself at the time of his conversion that he had no one to turn to for guidance and the Lord Himself taught him the way a schoolmaster teaches a little child. He finally got to a point where, even if all the Scriptures were destroyed, he would still hold on to what they revealed because of what the Lord had taught him personally.

Many Christians have not had the good fortune of Ignatius. We have, unfortunately, a surplus of people we can turn to for guidance. They badger us with their insistent teaching till we can barely hear the voice of our Lord Jesus through the din, even if we are listening. Karl Rahner tells of a Christian from India who prayed:

> It never occurred to me that I could get my knowledge firsthand from You, Lord, for they said to me, "We are all the teachers you will ever have; he who listens to us, listens to Him."
>
> But I'm not going to blame them or to deplore their presence in my life. It is I who am to blame. For I lacked the firmness to silence their voices; the courage to find out for myself; the determination to persist until You finally spoke; and the reckless confidence that someday, somewhere, You would break Your silence and speak to me.

Lacking that confidence, many committed Christians must acknowledge: "I have been content to learn about You at secondhand, Lord. From Scriptures and saints; from priests and preachers. I wish I could say to all of them, as the Samaritan villagers said to the woman who met Jesus at the well, "It's no longer because of what you said that I believe, for I have heard for myself."

Legalism is secondhand faith.

What does the way of reckless confidence mean in my own life today?

Reckless confidence for me is the unshakable conviction that Jesus and the Father love me in a way that defies imagination. It means to accept without reservation all that the Abba of Jesus has ordained for my life, to have the attitude of Jesus when He prayed in the garden, "Not My will but Yours be done," to make my own the prayer of Dag Hammarskjöld, "For all that has been, thanks. For all that shall be, yes."

Perhaps the only honest measure of the recklessness of my confidence is my readiness for martyrdom; my willingness not only to die for Him and the sake of the Gospel but to live for Him one day at a time.

The meaning of Easter is more than hope beyond the grave, more than the infallible guarantee that the resurrection of Jesus Christ is the pledge of my own. His Easter victory means first His sovereignty over the living as well as the dead. The risen Christ is Lord of my life right now, meaning He is God above all the gods of the unreal world out there—security, power, wealth, beauty or whatever else makes false claims on my life. Easter means for me empowerment to freedom, the freedom to be a living fulfillment of the first commandment, "I am the LORD your God. . . . You shall have no other gods before Me."

Every Easter brings to mind that beautiful story found in Nikolai Arseniew's book *Mysticism in the East.* Comrade Lunachatsky was lecturing in Moscow's largest assembly hall shortly after the Bolshevist Revolution. His theme was "religion: opium of the people." All the Christian mysteries are but myths, he said, supplanted by the light of science. Marxist science is the light that more than substitutes for the legends of Christianity. Lunachatsky spoke at great length. When he finished, he was so pleased with himself that he asked if anyone in the audience of some seven thousand had anything to add. A twenty-six-year-old Russian Orthodox priest, just ordained, stepped forward. First he apologized to the Commissar for his ignorance and awkwardness. The Commissar looked at him scornfully: "I'll give you two minutes, no more." "I won't take very long," the priest assured him. He mounted the platform, turned to the audience and in a loud voice declared, "Christ is risen!" As one man, that vast audience roared in response, "He is truly risen!"

May that response find an echo in your heart and mine because the resurrection of Jesus Christ from the dead is the source, the reason, the basis for the inarticulate joy of our Christian lives. Christ is risen, alleluia! He is Lord of the dance, the dance of the living. He is the Lord of laughter; our laughter is the echo of His risen life within us. He is the risen Lord of glory who in sovereign authority can say: "Blessed are you who laugh now, because you can bring the joy of Easter to others. But blessed are you only if you can laugh at yourselves, if you don't take yourselves too seriously, if human living doesn't revolve around you and your needs. Only if you can take delight in all of My Father's creation—in the sun and surf, in snow and star, in blue marlin and robin redbreast, in Cezanne, Olivia Newton John and veal scaloppine, in the love of a man or woman and in the presence of the living God within you. Only if your laughter means that you have let go in reckless confidence all that shackles you to yesterday, imprisons you in your small self today and frightens you with the uncertainty of tomorrow. Blessed are you who laugh, because you are free!"

FOR REFLECTION

Begin with five minutes of silent prayer, becoming aware in faith of God's indwelling presence and humbly asking the Spirit to speak to your heart through Scripture, personal reflection and the insights of others.

Let one of the group read aloud Luke 12:22–32. Then focus on the following questions for personal reflection and group interaction.

1. If you have internalized the mercy of Jesus, you are no longer plagued by unhealthy guilt, remorse and self-hatred. Share where you are and the measure of peace you have attained.
2. Share the psalm of thanksgiving you have written modeled on Psalm 103:1–5.
3. What, if any, are the traces of moralism/legalism remaining in your life?

CHAPTER 9

Lion and Lamb: The Relentless Tenderness of Jesus

An old Hasidic rabbi, Levi Yitzhak of Berdichev in the Ukraine, used to say that he discovered the meaning of love from a drunken peasant. Entering a tavern in the Polish countryside, he saw two peasants at a table, both gloriously in their cups. Each was protesting how much he loved the other, when Ivan said to Peter: "Peter, tell me what hurts me?" Bleary-eyed, Peter looked at Ivan: "How do I know what hurts you?" Ivan's answer was swift: "If you don't know what hurts me, how can you say you love me?"

The extraordinary perception and exquisite sensitivity of Jesus enabled Him to read the human heart with

piercing clarity. "He did not need man's testimony about
man, for he knew what was in a man" (John 2:25). Jesus
knew what hurt people. He knew then and He knows now.
He loves with a depth that escapes human comprehension. Several years ago, when a minister-friend of mine
bottomed out, resigned his church and abandoned his
family, he fled to a logging camp in New England. One
wintry afternoon as he sat shivering in his aluminum
trailer, the portable electric heater suddenly quit and
died. Cursing this latest evidence of a hostile universe,
the minister shouted, "God, I hate You!" then sank to his
knees weeping. There in the bright darkness of faith, he
heard Christ say, "I know; it's okay." Then this shattered
man heard Jesus weeping within him. The minister stood
up and started home.

The Lord is fine-tuned to the hates and loves, disap-
pointments and delights, brokenness and togetherness,
fears, joys and sorrows of each of us. That He knows what
hurts the human heart shows up all through His earthly
ministry: with the brokenhearted Magdalene crying at
His feet, the adulterous woman fearing for her life, the
Samaritan woman with her history of failed relationships, the women weeping along the road to Calvary. It
shows up in the many passages that describe Jesus as
"having compassion." The Greek verb *splangchnizomai*
is usually translated "to be moved with compassion." But
its etymological meaning is more profound and powerful.
The verb is derived from the noun *splangchna,* which
means intestines, bowels, entrails, that is to say, the
inward parts from which the strongest emotions arise.
In American argot, we would call it a gut reaction. That
is why English translations resort to active expressions
like "He was *moved* with pity" or "His heart *went out*
to them." But even these verbs do not capture the deep
physical flavor of the Greek word for compassion. The
compassion that Jesus felt was quite different from su-

perficial and ephemeral emotions of pity or sympathy. His heart was torn, His gut wrenched, the most vulnerable part of His being laid bare.

Henri Nouwen writes:

> It [*splangchnizomai*] is related to the Hebrew word for compassion, *rachamim,* which refers to the womb of Yahweh. Compassion is such a deep, central and powerful emotion in Jesus that it can only be described as a movement of the womb of God. There all the divine tenderness and gentleness lies hidden. There, God is father and mother, brother and sister, son and daughter. There, all feelings, emotions and passions are one in divine love.[1]

When Jesus wept within the brokenness of my minister-friend, the ground of all being shook, the source of all life trembled, the heart of all love burst open and the unfathomable depth of God's immense, inexhaustible caring revealed itself.

The numerous physical healings performed by Jesus to alleviate human suffering are only a hint of the anguish in the heart of God's Son for wounded humanity. His compassion surges from the bowels of His being and operates on a level that escapes human imitation. Jesus resonated with the depths of human sorrow. He became lost with the lost, hungry with the hungry and thirsty with the thirsty. On the cross He journeyed to the far reaches of loneliness, so that He could be lonely with those who are lonely and rob loneliness of its killing power by sharing it Himself.

He did then and He does now. Jesus vibrates to the hope and fear, the celebrations and desolations of each of us. He is the incarnation of the compassion of the Father. The fifteenth-century mystic Meister Eckhart wrote, "You may call God love, you may call God goodness, but the best name for God is compassion." When we speak of Jesus Christ as Emmanuel, God with us, we are saying that the greatest Lover in history knows what hurts us. Jesus reveals a God who is not indifferent to human agony, a God who fully embraces the human condition and plunges into the thick of our human struggle.

There is nothing that Jesus does not understand about the heartache that hangs like a cloud over the valley of history. In His own being He feels every separation and loss, every heart split open with grief, every cry of mourning down the corridors of time.

> To us who cry out from the depths of our brokenness for a hand that will touch us, an arm that can embrace us, lips that will kiss us, a word that speaks to us here and now, and a heart that is not afraid of our fears and tremblings; to us, who feel our own pain as no other human being feels it, has felt it, or ever will feel it and who are always waiting for someone who dares to come close—to us has come a man who can truly say, "I am with you." Jesus Christ is God with us and our every human pain reverberates in his innermost self.[2]

This is not pious piffle. The risen Jesus is not The Man Upstairs (as some macho males like to say), a celestial gas or the invisible honorary president of outer space. His resurrection was not an escape into the Great Beyond while the band played "Up, Up and Away." His breakthrough into new life on Easter morning unfettered Him from the space-time limitations of existence in the flesh and empowered Him to touch not only Nepal but New Orleans, not only Matthew and Magdalene but me. The Lion of Judah in His present risenness pursues, tracks and stalks us here and now. When we cry out with Jeremiah, "Enough already! Leave me alone in my melancholy," the Shepherd replies, "I will not leave you alone. You are Mine. I know each of My sheep by name.

You belong to Me. If you think I am finished with you, if you think I am a small god that you can keep at a safe distance, I will pounce upon you like a roaring lion, tear you to pieces, rip you to shreds and break every bone in your body. Then I will mend you, cradle you in My arms and kiss you tenderly."

The Lion and the Shepherd are one and the same. Ferocious pursuit and unwavering compassion are dual facts of the tremendous Lover who knows not only what hurts us but also how to heal us. And this savage and soothing God is also the Lamb who suffered the pains of death on our behalf. This was the experience of an old man who lay dying. When the priest came to anoint him, he noticed an empty chair at the man's bedside and asked him who had just been visiting. The sick man replied, "I place Jesus on that chair and I talk to Him." For years, he told the priest, he had found it extremely difficult to pray until a friend explained that prayer was just a matter of talking with Jesus. The friend suggested he imagine Jesus sitting in a chair where he could speak with Him and listen to what He said in reply. "I have had no trouble praying ever since."

Was the old man now sharing his fear of death, knowing that Jesus would feel what he was feeling? Was he agonizing over the grief his loved ones would experience, knowing that Jesus had been there? Was he praying for courage in the face of devouring death, knowing that Jesus sweated blood in the night?

Some days later, the daughter of this man came to the parish house to inform the priest that her father had just died. She said, "Because he seemed so content, I left him alone for a couple of hours. When I got back to the room, I found him dead. I noticed a strange thing, though: his head was resting not on the bed but on an empty chair that was beside his bed."[3]

The Lion who will kill all that separates us from Him; the Lamb who was killed to mend that separation—both

149

are symbols and synonyms for Jesus. Relentlessness and tenderness; indivisible aspects of the Divine Reality.

Why is the *splangchnizomai* (my free translation is "relentless tenderness") of Jesus so absent from our dealings with one another? Henri Nouwen has remarked: "When we take a critical look at ourselves, we have to recognize that *competition,* not compassion, is our main motivation in life."[4] This is a provocative insight. We are caught up in the game of one-upmanship. Our sense of self-worth depends upon how favorably or unfavorably we compare with others. Social climbing, power plays and the need to win rule out the possibility of compassion. Our sense of superiority is enhanced by the singular achievements we have scored.

We get possessive and protective of our trophies. Go to Brennan's house to envy his engraved invitation to the Presidential Prayer Breakfast with Ronnie and Nancy. It has been lacquered, laminated, spit-shined, enlarged to 40″ by 60″ and triumphantly staked on the front lawn with an overhanging spotlight for nighttime passersby. It makes him different from every neighbor on the street. After all, who am I if I cannot proudly point to something special that sets me apart from others? (I'm only kidding, of course: There is no monument to my uniqueness on our front lawn. Roslyn talked me out of it.)

This subtle spirit of competition, which reaches into the smallest corners of our relationships, prevents us from being compassionate. Compassion is a luxury I can afford only when confronted with something dramatic, like the Ethiopian crisis. Letting go of my distinct differences would mean losing my identity. (I mean, I would be just like everyone else, like the nondescript rabble who have never nibbled blueberry muffins with the president and the first lady.) Clearly, the call to compassionate living is unsettling, even threatening. The siren call of superiority, to be better tanned or better dressed, brighter or wealthier, more informed or competent than the next person, rings loud and clear within us.

But if the *splangchnizomai*—the relentless tenderness of Jesus—is to lay hold of us, our coherent sense of self must be rooted not in illusory differences but in our shared humanity. As we recovering alcoholics frequently say, "There, but for the grace of God, go I." Ignatius of Loyola said that one of the greatest graces he had ever received was the charism of the tax collector—the discovery that he was a sinner just like everyone else.

Early in his spiritual journey, the Trappist monk Thomas Merton wrote *Seeds of Contemplation,* in which he discreetly implied that mystics were a breed apart. Later he was so stunned by the revelation of his solidarity with sinners, his unalloyed inclusion in the human family, that he cried out: "This sense of liberation from illusory differences was such a relief and such a joy to me that I almost laughed out loud. . . . Thank God, thank God that I am like other men, that I am only a man among others. It is a glorious destination to be a member of the human race."[5]

The relentless tenderness of Jesus challenges us to give up our false faces, our petty conceits, our irritating vanities, our preposterous pretending, and become card-carrying members of the messy human community. Jesus calls us to be tender with each other because He is tender. He invites us into the fellowship of saved sinners wherein our identity and glory lie not in titles, trinkets, honorary degrees and imaginary differences but in our "new self" in Christ irrevocably bonded to our brothers and sisters in the family of God.

As the first letter of Peter puts it, we are "partakers of the divine nature," caught up in the very life of God Himself, enabled to transcend our automatic emotions of fear and distaste and all the judgmental junk we carry, empowered to be unrelentingly tender as the Lion-Lamb is relentless and tender.

And His compassion knows no frontiers or boundaries and extends to all. Even to myself.

One of the most shocking contradictions in Christian living is the intense dislike many disciples of Jesus have for themselves. They are more displeased, impatient, irritated, unforgiving and spiteful with their own shortcomings than they would ever dream of being with someone else's. They are fed up with themselves, sick of their own mediocrity, disgusted by their own inconsistency, bored by their own monotony. They would never judge any other of God's children with the savage self-condemnation with which they crush themselves. Through experiencing the relentless tenderness of Jesus, we learn first of all to be gentle with ourselves. To the extent that we allow the *splangchnizomai* of the Lord to invade our hearts, we are freed from the dyspepsia toward ourselves that follows us everywhere, that self-hatred that we are now even ashamed of. It is simply not possible to know the Christ of the Gospels unless we alter our attitude toward ourselves and take sides with Him, against our own self-evaluation. Would you like to know this moment how Jesus feels about you? Bernard Bush says this is the way you will know: If you love yourself intensely and freely, then your feelings about yourself correspond perfectly to the sentiments of Jesus.

And the divine double take, of course, is that loving ourselves frees us to love others. There's a passage in the novel *The Face Beside the Fire* that I have been unable to get out of my mind. Laurens Van der Post describes an insecure woman in fierce competition with her husband. To avoid revealing her vulnerability, she foregoes tenderness. "Slowly she is poisoning Albert [with a] poison . . . found in no chemist's shop. . . . It is a poison brewed from all the words, the delicate, tender, burning trivialities and petty endearments she's never used."[6] The love we withhold through our power struggles in marriage and in our relationships is liberated through our union with Jesus. It is a new way of living in which comparisons, contrasts, rivalries, competition and power trips are gradually left behind.

This is what Paul means by "a new creation," by our minds being renewed in a spiritual revolution. We are never more like Jesus than when we are choked with compassion for others. In writing this chapter I have been deeply moved. Martin Luther said, "The Word should shape the interior existence of the preacher"—in this case the author. The relentless tenderness of the Lion-Lamb for me makes me tremble with wonder and joy. I experience awe, certitude, thanksgiving, what the French call *joie debordante* and a deep sense of reverence. At the same time I am humbled, convicted and challenged by my own lack of it. I am grieved by my calibrated compassion, my measured affection, the terms of endearment I have withheld from my spouse, children, parents, friends and hurting acquaintances . . . until such time as they fulfill my expectations.

However, the Lord Jesus is not calling me to self-condemnation and unhealthy guilt. Self-centered guilt closes me in upon myself and preempts the presence of a compassionate God. I should not be shocked and horrified that I have failed. Jesus certainly isn't. In His boundless mercy that keeps no score of wrongs, He calls me to repentance, to humbly acknowledge my failure without being unduly disturbed by it, and in the power of His Spirit to get on with the compassionate life. His word to me today is the word He spoke to Peter after his triple denial, "Shalom, My friend, Shalom." In the peace of Christ, the words of Francis of Assisi on his deathbed echo within me: "Let us begin, my brothers, for up to now we have done but little."

The *splangchnizomai* of Jesus helps me to nail down the meaning of the most mangled and manipulated word

153

in the English language—*love*. Dr. James Shannon put it vividly: We use "love" to describe "the motive for the voluntary death of Jesus Christ on Calvary, the subject matter of hard pornographic movies, the bond of affection between Flower children, the intimate union of husband and wife, and the unbuttoned promiscuity of Fire Island on a weekend."[7]

The compassionate love of Jesus at work within us is an empowering to suffer with, endure with, struggle with, partake of, be moved in the depths of our being for the hunger, nakedness, loneliness, pain, squalid choices and failed dreams of our brothers and sisters in the human family. We don't have to join mission works in places unknown to us. The passion of Christ is being played out in our own communities, perhaps in our own homes, in anyone who is in agony of flesh or spirit. Jesus is there not in some vague, eerie way but as a real presence—for what we do for the least of our brothers and sisters, we do for Him. On that Calvary next door where Christ still hangs, I will minister to my Savior and my Lord.

The *splangchnizomai* of Jesus leaves no room for otherworldly idealism or sentimental piety. Biblically, compassion means action. I'm thinking of a poster popular in the sixties, "Love is a verb." A tear shed for a lonely widow is a mere emotion; when combined with writing her a letter, knocking on her door or dialing her on the telephone, it is compassion. The difference is trenchantly described in 1 John 3:17–18: "If anyone has material possessions and sees his brother in need but has no pity on him, how can the love of God be in him? Dear children, let us not love with words or tongue but with actions and in truth."

Every time the Gospels mention that Jesus was moved with the deepest emotions, they go on to describe His doing something—feeding the hungry crowds, interceding with God, bringing physical or inner healing, deliverance or exorcism. The Good Samaritan was commended precisely because he acted. The priest and the Levite, paragons of correct theological understanding, flunked the crucial test because they didn't do anything.

The unglamorous and little-publicized words of mercy, the ministry of small things, feeding and sheltering, visiting the sick and incarcerated, educating, correcting, speaking a healing word, bearing wrongs, listening creatively, counseling, washing dirty feet, praying with people, are all ways of living the life of compassion. This is no minor matter. When Jesus tells us in Matthew 5:48, "Be perfect . . . as your heavenly Father is perfect," the same commandment is translated in Luke 6:36 (JB): "Be compassionate as your Father is compassionate."

Matthew Fox says: "Compassion is a spirituality of meat, not milk, of adults, not children; of love, not masochism; of justice, not philanthropy. It requires maturity, a big heart, a willingness to risk, and imagination."

In this book I have spoken frequently of my own glimpse of Jesus. A glimpse is a glimpse, a partial view, and nothing more. And nothing less. The Jesus of my journey, the way He has revealed Himself to me, is as the Compassionate One. Compassionate not because He is the Son of God, but Son of God because He is compassionate beyond mortal possibility. Therein lies His divinity for me. He is the image of the invisible God. Should you choose to call Jesus goodness, He will be good to you; should you choose to call Him love, He will be loving to you; should you choose to call Him compassion, He will know that you know.

Laurens Van der Post relates the story of two brothers. The elder brother was strong, tall, intelligent, an excellent athlete. Sent away to a private school in South Africa where the family lived, he became an admired leader of the student body. His brother was some six years younger. Neither good-looking nor capable, he was also a hunchback. But he had one great gift. He had a magnificent singing voice. I found it easy to identify

155

with this story as I was such a younger brother (even though I couldn't sing).

Eventually the younger brother joined the older at the same boarding school. One day in a cruel outbreak of mob psychology, a group of students ganged up on the younger brother, jeered at him and tore off his shirt to reveal his hunchback.

The older brother was aware of what was going on. He could have gone out and faced the crowd of sadistic students, acknowledged the strange hunchback as his brother and put a stop to the whole sorry mess. Instead, he remained in the chemistry lab completing an assignment. He betrayed his brother by what he failed to do.

The younger brother was never the same again. He returned home to his parents' farm where he kept to himself and sang no more. Meanwhile the older brother had become a soldier in World War II, stationed in Palestine. One night, lying outdoors and gazing into the starlit sky, he realized what he had done to his younger brother in their school days. His heart told him that he would never have peace until he went home and asked his brother for forgiveness. And so he made the incredibly difficult wartime journey from Palestine to South Africa. The brothers talked long into the night, the older one confessing his guilt and remorse. They cried together, embraced, and the breach between them was healed.

Something else happened that night. The older brother had fallen asleep when he was startled awake by the sound of a full, rich, mellifluous voice soaring into the night. It was the beautiful voice of his younger brother who was singing once again.[8]

By one costly, concrete act of compassionate caring, the older brother brought healing and wholeness to his brother, to himself and to the relationship. Perhaps the ultimate betrayal of the *splangchnizomai* of Jesus is the failure to love when we have the opportunity to do so. Forgive me if I use these final lines to examine my own conscience, but I am asking myself some hard and honest questions about this book I am writing. Does it reveal intransigent rebellion against the unfairness of the system that disqualifies a married man from ministry in the Roman Catholic Church? Have I allowed my pain to harden into unforgiveness? Have I communicated a smug superiority over certain legalistic preachers? Have I betrayed my own inner word—that compassion is the only reality, that all else is illusion, misconception, falsehood? Of one thing I am certain: Compassion is the name by which Jesus has revealed Himself to me, and my own identity becomes ambiguous, tentative and confused whenever I allow anything but the relentless tenderness of the Lion-Lamb of God to dictate my perception of reality—be it self-righteous anger, defensiveness, the desire to win, the pressing need to change others, carping criticism, a gnawing hunger for vindication, frustration at the blindness of others, whatever. Am I in harmony with myself or alienated from the real me?

The prayerful reflection and soul-searching involved in writing this chapter have been a gift of God to me, an experience of catharsis, inner healing, insight, challenge and peace. I pray that the Lion of Judah who is the Lamb of God has spoken to the inner sanctuary of your heart as well. As you close this chapter I ask our Father that you be led by the Spirit *to set free the song* that sleeps in the wounded flesh of a brother or sister.

As H. L. Mencken said, it might be as simple as winking at a homely girl.

FOR REFLECTION

Begin with five minutes of silent prayer, becoming aware in faith of God's indwelling presence and humbly

157

asking the Spirit to speak to your heart through Scripture, personal reflection and the insights of others.

Let one of the group read aloud Matthew 11:25–27. Then focus on the following questions for personal reflection and group interaction.

1. Commenting on the three temptations by Satan in the desert, Henri Nouwen wrote: "The three temptations were three ways to seduce Jesus into becoming a competitor for love. The world of the tempter was precisely that world in which people compete for love through doing useful, sensational and powerful things and so winning medals that gain them affection and admiration."[9] Are you competing for love through acts of kindness and service, hoping to win affection and approval through your good deeds? In other words, are you doing the right thing for the wrong reason?

2. Is your mind giving to things the importance they have in reality?

3. Does the Jesus of your journey love you when you are good and reject you when you are bad?

JESUS
AT CHRISTMAS

CHAPTER 10

The $\mathcal{G}$reat Season of $\mathcal{H}$ope

Once a year the Christmas season strikes both the sacred and secular spheres of life with sledgehammer force: Suddenly Jesus Christ is everywhere.

For approximately one month His presence is inescapable. You may accept Him or reject Him, affirm Him or deny Him, but you cannot ignore Him. Of course He is proclaimed in speech, song and symbol in all the Christian churches. But He rides every red-nosed reindeer, lurks behind every new doll, resonates in the most desacralized "season's greetings." Remotely or proximately, He is toasted in every cup of Christmas cheer. Each sprig of holly is a hint of His holiness, each cluster of mistletoe a sign He is here.

For those who claim His name, Christmas heralds this luminous truth: The God of Jesus Christ is our absolute future. Such is the deeply hopeful character of this sacred season. By God's free doing in Bethlehem, nothing can separate us from the love of God in Christ Jesus. Light, life and love are on our side.

The Christmas story was written in the light of post-paschal faith. The infancy narratives in Matthew and Luke can be dismissed as quaint stories if Jesus is not risen. If He is, the long dream of Israel has come true and the messianic era has erupted into history. Similarly, the Sermon on the Mount can be safely praised as a magnificent ethic, if Christ is not risen. If He is, praise does not matter. It is a portrait of our ultimate destiny. It is appropriate, then, to reflect on the Christmas mystery, as the evangelists did, *after* Easter rather than before.

"Jesus Christmases in us whenever people come home to themselves in our presence, and when they feel a little less hopeful and joyful because we are absent." These words, scribbled in a journal several years ago in solitude, lay hold of me with prophetic power when the great season of hope begins. Christians are a people of hope to the extent that others can find in us a source of strength and joy. If not, our profession of faith "By the power of the Holy Spirit He was born of the Virgin Mary and became man" is as academic, tentative and hopeless as the alcoholic who promises, "I'll quit tomorrow." To know means to be transformed by what one knows.

The story goes that Thomas Aquinas, perhaps the world's greatest theologian, toward the end of his life suddenly stopped writing. When his secretary complained that his work was unfinished, Thomas replied: "Brother Reginald, when I was at prayer a few months ago, I experienced something of the reality of Jesus Christ. That day, I lost all appetite for writing. In fact, all I have ever written about Christ seems now to me to be like straw."

When the scholar becomes a mystic, that is, someone who has experienced something, he discovers that he has nothing to say. He can only stutter and stammer. All of his hard-won learning is straw. When the Most High God reveals Himself through the vulnerability of an infant, I must listen: I have nothing to teach, nothing to say.

> The attempt to reduce the Lord Jesus to a manageable size is a common but fatal error. It robs Him of His *Otherness* and confines Him to the world of our mental limits. Aquinas warned against this: "If you comprehend God, He is not God." In the same vein the Zen Master says, "If you meet the Buddha, kill the Buddha." That is, if you think you have comprehended the Buddha, destroy your comprehension of him. The secret is to know that *"The Son of God is always greater."* No matter how great we think Him to be, He is always greater.[1]

The reflections that follow are no more than straw from the stable, the stuttering of a sinful, shipwrecked man who has often let go of the plank and through whom God still continues to work. This self-assessment is not only honest, it is consoling and freeing for anyone caught up in the oppression of thinking that God can work only through saints. What a word of healing, forgiveness and comfort it is for many of us Christians who have discovered that we are earthen vessels, that before the cock crowed twice, we had let go of the plank three times.

I come to the stable just as I am, not as I should be (since I'm never going to be as I should be), a poor, weak, sinful man with easy rationalizations for my inconsistent behavior, a little frightened because I am called to live out the words I am setting down on paper. The little Child looks at me, smiles and says: "Don't be afraid; I am with you. I expect more failure from you than you expect from yourself. Peace is My gift to you. Live this day in the wisdom of accepted tenderness."

No one has made this more real to me than my wife, Roslyn. She has come to know all my flaws and faults and character defects and seems not to notice. Or if she does, she doesn't get as upset as I do. She loves me not in spite of my faults (that wouldn't be real acceptance, I guess) but with them. St. Augustine said, "A friend is someone who knows everything about you and still loves you." Roslyn has brought the compassion and tenderness of Jesus Christ very near to me.

One of the many documented miracles that have occurred in Lourdes, France, took place in 1957. A French father took his ten-year-old son, blind from birth, on a pilgrimage from Britany to Lourdes. At the shrine, the child begged his father to pray for him. His dad prayed aloud, "Lord, give my boy his sight." Instantly the boy could see. He looked around. He saw flowers, trees, green grass, the open sky. Then he looked into his father's eyes, the eyes that went with the only voice he had known during ten long years of darkness and loneliness.

When he saw his father, do you know what he said?

"Oh boy. Everybody's here!"

This is the spirit of Christmas. Everybody's here! The deep, passionate love of Jesus Christ, our Lord and brother, is the breakthrough of Bethlehem and the heartbeat of the Christian life.

The Abba of Jesus says:

Make ready for My Christ,
whose smile
like lightning
sets free the song of everlasting glory
that now sleeps in your paper flesh like dynamite.

In His wisdom and mercy, God can use even straw, a thing of trifling value and consequence, to serve His purpose. If the straw I have found in the stable leads to

Christmasing and homecoming in one human heart, the writing of this book has accomplished its purpose.

FOR REFLECTION

Begin with five minutes of silent prayer, becoming aware in faith of God's indwelling presence and humbly asking the Spirit to speak to your heart through Scripture, personal reflection and the insights of others.

Let one of the group read aloud Philippians 3:7–14. Then focus on the following questions for personal reflection and group interaction.

1. With the numerous demands made on your time in December, are you able to maintain the priorities of God, family and work or ministry?
2. Comment on the short paragraph "Jesus Christmases in us . . ."
3. Have you expressed your sensitivity to the poor in the days preceding Christmas?

CHAPTER 11

The Crisis
of Christmas

The crisis of Christmas in the Christian community, put bluntly, is a crisis of *faith*. Faith is a commitment to Truth, who is Jesus Christ. Faith is dedication to Reality, who is Jesus Christ. When my mind gives to things the importance they have in reality, I am living in the truth. But when the social conventions, artificial distractions and superficial claims of the unreal world, which is passing away, dominate my time, interest and attention, I am living in untruth.

The primitive confession of faith "Jesus is Lord" is not an abstract theological proposition but a highly personal statement. It puts my integrity on the line and profoundly affects the way I celebrate Advent, the four weeks of preparation for the birth of Christ. If Jesus is Lord of *my* life and *my* Christmas, I am challenged to

167

submit all the priorities of my personal and professional life to this primary fact.

Paraphrasing Paul in his letter to the Ephesians, "You must lay aside your old self and your former way of celebrating Christmas . . . and acquire a fresh spiritual way of thinking."

The traditional hymn sung in many churches on Sunday morning, "Christ Jesus Victor, Christ Jesus *Ruler,* Christ Jesus Lord and Redeemer," implies that the relationship with Jesus is the most intense and intimate of all my relations. Is this really true? In gut-level honesty, what rules our lives as we prepare for Christmas? What has power over us?

First, I suppose, it's people. Those who speak to me; the men and women whose words I read. Those with whom I associate or would like to associate; those who give to me and those who refuse; those who help and those who hinder; those whom I like and those whom I do not like. Such people occupy my attention, fill my thoughts, in a sense, *rule* in me.

Jesus Christ? Well, He counts, but only after I have finished with the others. Only when they and their claims leave me time for Him. Sometimes these others occupy so much of my time that the whole day slips by without a thought of the Lord of my life. Even at worship, I can be so distracted by my friends and enemies that I forget to lift up my mind and heart to Him. Oh, I may recite a few mechanical prayers, but my thoughts are somewhere else. "This people gives me lip service," Isaiah heard the God of Israel say, "but their heart is far from me." Like King Claudius in Shakespeare's *Hamlet:* "My words fly up, my thoughts remain below; words without thoughts never to heaven go."

What else rules in me besides people? *Things*—things I desire. Money, popularity, power, personal appearance, a Mercedes convertible. Also the *problems* that preoccupy me—the future, the past, career advancement, my neighbor's bad breath, a thousand trivial concerns. These fill the spiritual space within me, not Jesus. He is present to me only when the crowding, all-absorbing pressures of my little world leave room for Him. No, Jesus does not dominate my life. Any tree in my path seems to have more power than He, if only because it forces me to walk around it! So much of my life is illusory because my values and my mind-set belong to an unreal world. What would life be like if Christ did rule in me? If during Advent my primary concern were His Kingdom?

But what rules in me is the kingdom of people, the kingdom of events, petty plans and personal interests. They stifle Jesus Christ, crowd Him out of my life. Who can understand how Jesus can be the Son of God and I can be so indifferent to Him? What shape would Advent and Christmas take if Jesus really *ruled* in me?

If He did, that is, if my faith were deep, burning, powerful and passionate, my life would be very different. My self-esteem would cease to be based upon the worldly values of possessions, prestige, status and privilege, and upon the group solidarities of family, race, class, religion and nation. For to make these my supreme values is to have nothing in common with Jesus. With burning faith I would speak of Jesus not as some distant being but as a close friend with whom I have a personal relationship. The invisible world would become more real than the invisible, the world of what I believe more real than the world of what I see, Christ more real than myself. Christmas would be more than a breathless finale to a frantic shopping season, more than sentimental music, tinsel on the tree, a liturgical pageant and boozy goodwill toward the world. Yes, life would be radically different if Jesus Christ ruled in me, if my faith had the force of a passionate conviction.

But my life *must* be different. To be a Christian means to stake one's life on the revelation of God in Jesus Christ. In the early church Jesus made such a profound impact on His followers that they found it impossible to believe that anyone could be equal to Him—not Moses or Elijah or even Abraham. And the idea that a prophet or judge or messiah should come after Jesus and be even greater was simply inconceivable. It was not necessary to wait for someone else. Jesus was everything. If anyone was to judge the world at the end, it must be Jesus. If anyone was to be acknowledged as Lord, King, Messiah, Son of God, how could it be anyone but Jesus?

> The early Christians' admiration and veneration for Jesus knew no bounds. He was in every way the ultimate, the only criterion of good and evil, of truth and falsehood, the only hope for the future, the only power which could transform the world. Jesus was experienced as *the* definitive breakthrough in the history of man. He transcended everything that had ever been said and done before. He was in every way the ultimate, the last word. He was on a par with God. His word was God's Word. His Spirit was God's Spirit. His feelings were God's feelings. What He stood for was exactly the same as what God stood for. No higher esteem was conceivable.[1]

To believe in Jesus in 2004 is to cry *Amen!* to the perception, assessment and evaluation of the early Christians. Jesus is the truth, He is reality, He is Lord.

It stands to reason that if during the Advent season we relegate Jesus and what He stands for to second place on our scale of values, then we have already denied Him and what He stands for. Either you accept the Kingdom as Jesus understood it or you don't. You cannot serve two masters. It is all or nothing. Second place or half measures are tantamount to nothing. To believe in Jesus is to believe that Jesus is divine, that He is the Son of God.

Turn the pages of the Gospels: If there is anything that Jesus is absolutely insistent upon, one thing that is indispensable and unequivocal, it is the *necessity* of faith. The Lord never lifted a finger to help anyone unless He first saw their faith. Remember the two blind men on the road to Jericho crying, "Have mercy on us, Son of David!" In this unforgettable scene in chapter 9 of Matthew's Gospel, Jesus replies, "Do you believe I am able to do this?" They answer, "Yes, Lord." Only then does He touch their eyes: "According to your faith will it be done to you."

Recall how Jesus could not work any miracles in His hometown of Nazareth *because the people there did not believe in Him.*

In chapter 15 of Matthew, Jesus heals the daughter of a non-Jew: "Woman, you have great faith! Your request is granted." And when His own disciples ask Him why they were unable to cast out a demon, Jesus answers, "Because you have so little faith" (Matthew 17:20).

Within His inner circle, Jesus never allowed veneration, love, affection or admiration to substitute for faith. Though He loved Martha and Mary and their dead brother dearly, Jesus demanded an answer before He restored Lazarus to life: "He who believes in me will live, even though he dies. . . . Do you believe this?" (John 11:25–26).

There is no need to multiply examples of what is so patently an essential condition of the Christian walk. We are saved through faith—an unflagging, unwavering attachment to the person of Jesus Christ.

What is the depth and quality of your faith commitment? Is it a halfhearted intellectual assent to a dusty pawnshop of doctrinal beliefs? In the last analysis, faith is not a way of speaking or even of thinking; it is a way of living. Maurice Blondel said, "If you want to know what a person really believes, don't listen to what he says but watch what he does." Only the practice of faith can verify what we believe. Does faith permeate the whole of your life? Does it form your judgments about death? About success? Does it influence the way you read the newspaper? Do you have a divine sense of humor that sees through people and events into the unfolding plan of God? When things are turbulent on the surface of your life, do you retain a quiet calm, firmly fixed in ultimate reality? As Therese of Lisieux said, "Let nothing disturb you, let nothing frighten you. All things are passing. God alone remains." Does your faith shape your Advent season this year?

Jesus paints a striking portrait of the different levels of faith commitment: "A farmer went out to sow his seed. As he was scattering the seed, some fell along the path, and the birds came and ate it up. Some . . . sprang up quickly. . . . But when the sun came up, the plants were scorched, and they withered because they had no root. Other seed fell among thorns, which grew up and choked the plants. Still other seed fell on good soil, where it produced a crop—a hundred, sixty or thirty times what was sown. He who has ears, let him hear" (Matthew 13:3–9).

In this haunting parable, Jesus depicts four different groups of people exposed to the Word of God. First come the *insensitive*. They hear the Word, but it does not speak to them interiorly. The unseen world does not exist for the thinking man. The tales of the Bible are nice for children but not for mature adults. Faith is an outdated conception for those behind the times, a relic of the Middle Ages. After all, you can't pay the rent with religion. It's muscles that decide, and intelligence, and connections, and stronger battalions. All else is opium for the people. For the insensitive the Word of God is meaningless. At most it hits the external ear and bounces off. The number of the insensitive is legion.

Next, Jesus describes the *superficial.* These are the open people—too much so. They are ready to receive everything, but nothing takes root. You meet them at every level of the church's life, exponents of change for the sake of change. Ardent champions of renewal and reform with a lusty contempt for anything written before 1963. These are the butterfly types who sip on a thousand different blossom cups. Sanguine people of the moment—today elated to the sky and tomorrow depressed to the point of death. Their laugh fades quickly and their tears dry still faster. Of course they have their devout moments. The superficial get a warm feeling at the ringing of church bells and a wave of nostalgia at the odor of incense. In the home hangs a cross or crucifix, with the Holy Bible nearby. Just don't subject them to endurance tests. Let no sacrifice challenge their faith commitment. Never intimate that the cost of discipleship is high and in the days ahead it may be exorbitant. In times of testing they hide their Bible and bury their cross. Weathervane people who cannot be trusted—their number too is legion.

The third group are the *defeated.* They may have fought long and struggled honorably for their faith. They had principles they wanted to live by. A Christian ethic was presumed, a week without worship unthinkable. Their high ideals, however, ran into competition from "the real world." Love of God got swallowed up in mundane concerns. The thorny preoccupations are many—career, romance, military induction, geographical displacement, progeny, security. The Lordship of Jesus Christ is slowly strangled by alien growths. Cut off from light and nourishment, it asserts itself less and less and in the end succumbs to spiritual asphyxiation.

Finally, Jesus speaks of the *victorious*—the seeds that fell on rich soil. But even here Jesus distinguishes three levels of productivity for the Kingdom, three different degrees of faith commitment among genuine hearers of

173

the Word of God. The 30-percenters, the 60-percenters and the 100-percenters.

The 30-percenter is often a pillar of the church. He is involved in church-related activities and organizations. He reads a Christian newspaper or magazine. He prays daily. He finds personal security and reassurance in rituals, devotions and prayer meetings. These structures provide a measure of peace and allow his life to move on undisturbed. He shrinks, however, from the more radical demands of the Gospel. He may take refuge in legalism, morality and an artificially closed circle of thought and practice. The 30-percenters help build an agreeable world of nice people. But the fire of Francis of Assisi and the passion of Mary Magdalene are foreign to their experience.

The 60-percenter is genuinely other-centered. He holds doors for people, he would stop on the road to help someone change a flat tire, he works on community projects. He never cuts people down. He believes that this is what it means to be a Christian. He applauds church reform and renewal. He has read all the right Christian authors. He likes experimental forms of worship. He doesn't accept automatically what is told to him by the institutional church, preferring to think things through for himself. He insists that Christianity be "meaningful and relevant."

His greatest strength lies in his conviction that "being Christian" means loving others. There are two types here—the personalists and the social activists. The personalist believes that personal relationships are the essence of the Gospel message. He favors the dialogue sermon, the sign of peace and the coffee and donuts afterward. He reads and rereads the Scriptures emphasizing our relationships one to another. The social activist wants all people to become fully human and quotes the words of St. Irenaeus, "The glory of God is man fully alive."

What is the one thing missing in the 60-percenter? Passionate faith in the divinity of Jesus Christ. He has not surrendered to the mystery of the fire of the Spirit that burns within. He stays close enough to the fire to keep warm but never plunges in; he does not come out burnt and incandescently transformed. He is a nicer man than most with better morals than most but not a *brand-new creation.*

His religion is good and noble but *inadequate* because it mistakes elements of Christianity for the whole. It is admirable and praiseworthy to support the church, obey the commandments, stay updated theologically and love other people. Obviously these are excellent goals and borne of the Gospel. But to the extent that they become absolutes, faith commitment is impoverished and the Gospel message devaluated.

The 100-percenter hears the Word of God and understands it as a summons to faith in the person of Jesus Christ. "Jesus is God's own Son!" That is the staggering, mind-blowing ecstatic profession of faith of the 100-percenter. It is the same primitive confession of the early church—"Jesus is Lord." It is the fiery faith of Paul whose life was *ruled* by one desire: "I consider everything a loss compared to the surpassing greatness of knowing Christ Jesus my Lord, for whose sake I have lost all things. I consider them rubbish, that I may gain Christ" (Philippians 3:8).

The full life of faith becomes reality when a Christian is laid waste by one pure passion.

Nikos Kazantzakis tells the story of a thirsty Moslem who came upon a well in the desert. He dropped a bucket into the well and pulled it up. It was full of silver. Emptying the bucket, he dumped it into the well again and pulled it up full of gold. The Moslem protested: "My Lord God, I know how powerful you are and what marvels you are capable of. But all I want is a cup of water." He emptied the bucket of gold, lowered it into the well, and retrieved it. It was full of water. He drank and quenched his thirst.[2]

That is to be laid waste, devastated by one passion. That is purity of heart.

The Christian who yields a hundredfold wants Jesus Christ and wants to want nothing else. He has directed his whole life to seeking Jesus, to developing a personal relationship with Him, to growing into a more intimate and heartfelt knowledge of Him. Jesus Christ is literally the most important person in his life. He allows the Christ to be Lord of his life not simply by agreeing with all the intellectual doctrines about Him but by turning his life over to Jesus.

In doing so, he realizes that Jesus wants him not only when he is strong, on top, unafraid, invulnerable to Satan and in control of every situation. This is the attitude of the 30-percenters and the 60-percenters—they have to be perfect or at least very good before they believe Jesus will accept them. That is because they do not know Him. The faith-filled Christian is constantly turning to Jesus for forgiveness. Disgust at his own feebleness and failure only redoubles his trust and dependence on his Lord.

The 100-percenter knows with his heart as well as his head that the Kingdom of God has come in Jesus Christ—that *now* is the hour of salvation. He knows that the Master stands at the crossroads of his life. The urgency of the moment demands commitment-decision. Drop everything and run for Christ. Like when a tornado comes ripping down the street. You can't postpone a decision. You can't procrastinate. This is the salvific now. Leave your mother and father, mutilate yourself for the Kingdom, pluck out your eye, cut off your hand, but for Christ's sake, for the love of Jesus Christ, don't let the invitation go unanswered. What does the loss of reputation, popularity, status, life itself mean in comparison with the gain of Christ Jesus? The greatest moment in history has come and is rushing forward toward its conclusion. Open up! This is not an Avon salesperson at the door. It is the Son of God. His invitation is to be treated with unconditional seriousness.

What distinguishes the Christian whose faith is deep, burning, powerful and luminous is just this *seriousness*. Seriousness is not the opposite of joy but of superficiality. Francis of Assisi was such a lighthearted, whimsical, musical, gentle man. But that was only part of his character. On the other side was the totally dedicated, unbending, relentless search for truth and reality. He was a Jesus-haunted man who gave up all to obtain all. His seriousness changed him from the wealthy son of a comfortable Umbrian home into the blind ragged beggar of Mount Alvernia. It was his seriousness about what he read in the Gospel that turned his life into what it was.

The crisis of Christmas in the Christian community is truly a crisis of faith. Many of us will continue to ignore the invitation, dodge the truth, evade reality and postpone the decision about Jesus—which is a decision itself.

Yet Christmas is the birthday of the Son of God. What will separate the men from the boys, the women from the girls, the mystics from the romantics next Christmas will be the depth and quality of our passion for Jesus. The insensitive will eat, drink and be merry; the superficial will follow social customs in a religious setting; the defeated will be haunted by ghosts from the past.

And the victorious minority who are not intimidated by the cultural patterns of the lockstepping, anonymous and unbelieving majority will celebrate as though He is near, near in time, near in place, the witness of our motives, our speech, our behavior. As indeed He is.

The world will ignore them. A few pious and proper Christians may call them religious fanatics. But the victorious will be in touch with truth and living in reality. Their passion and seriousness about Christmas will be a microcosm, a paradigm, a foretaste of their life in Christ Jesus through the coming year.

The contemplatives will be among their numbers. So will the shipwrecked. And you and I? How are we going to celebrate Christmas?

FOR REFLECTION

Begin with five minutes of silent prayer, becoming aware in faith of God's indwelling presence and humbly asking the Spirit to speak to your heart through Scripture, personal reflection and the insights of others.

Let one of the group read aloud Mark 6:1–6. Then focus on the following questions for personal reflection and group interaction.

1. In the commentary on the parable of the sower and the seed, at which level do you place yourself? If level four, are you at 30, 60 or 100 percent?
2. When life gets turbulent, when someone attributes to you motives that you do not have, when you experience loneliness, rejection by a friend, sudden unemployment or a bout of depression, are you able to maintain a quiet inner calm through the awareness that God loves you as you are and not how you should be?
3. Intensity of desire is of paramount importance in the life of prayer. Has your desire for intimacy with Jesus intensified since you were saved?

CHAPTER 12

The Contemplative at Christmas

One of the handful of books that have had a profound impact on my life is the late Paul Tillich's *The Shaking of the Foundations*. It contains this passage:

> To be struck by grace does not mean that we are simply making progress in our moral self-control, in our fight against special faults, and in our relationships to others. Moral progress may be a fruit of grace, but it is not grace itself.
>
> Grace strikes us when we are in great pain and restlessness. It strikes us when we walk through the dark valley of a meaningless and empty life. . . . Grace strikes us when our disgust for our own being, our indifference, our weakness, our hostility, and our lack of direction and composure have become intolerable to us.
>
> Sometimes at that moment a wave of light breaks into our darkness and it is as though a voice were saying: "You are accepted. You are accepted by that which

is greater than you. . . . Do not seek for anything; do not perform anything; do not intend anything. *Simply accept the fact that you are accepted.*"

If that happens to us, we experience grace. After such an experience we may not be better than before, and we may not believe more than before. But everything is transformed.[1]

Such an experience is not the result of reasoning or spiritual striving. It is a fruit of the Spirit that normally matures in *prayer* in which the awareness of God's acceptance is discovered and later deepened. It is one thing to know Jesus Christ loves us and another thing to *realize* it. In prayer we discover what we already have. You start from where you are and realize that you are already there. We already have everything, but many of us don't know it and therefore don't experience it. Everything has been given to us by the Father in Jesus. All we need now is to experience what we already possess. The most precious moments of prayer consist in letting ourselves be loved by the Lord.

During the Christmas season we don't have to seek after God in prayer. We could not seek Him unless we had already found Him. Abba, Jesus and the Spirit have been there all the time, and if we create the opportunity in prayer, God will make Himself known to us. "We learn to pray," said the late Thomas Merton, "by praying."

In our technological world the word *mystic* has fallen on hard times. Used mostly in a pejorative sense, a "mystic" has come to mean someone who is spaced out in a dreamy metaphysical fog. An authentic mystic, however, is not a person who engages in unusual forms of prayers accompanied by visions, ecstasies and levitations. A mystic, in the words of the German theologian Karl Rahner, is someone who has experienced something. A mystic is aglow with passionate longing for Jesus Christ who is sought, loved and worshiped for Himself alone. *A mystic is a person whose life is ruled by thirst.* That thirst is slaked in prayer, in the knowing-loving-and-delighting in a person. "This is eternal life: that they may know you, the only true God, and Jesus Christ, whom you have sent" (John 17:3).

The contemplative at Christmas grows quiet before "the light [that] shines in the darkness" (John 1:5). He stills his soul and becomes tranquil like a child in its mother's arms. He interiorizes and appropriates to himself the mercy, forgiveness, reconciliation and love that are embodied in the Child of Bethlehem. He surrenders to the grace of the Word made flesh. He accepts acceptance.

Contemplating the crib (meaning, looking at Jesus while loving Him), the Christian's faith flames into joyous expectation that the Christ who came in history will one day come in glory. Paul writes in Colossians: "When Christ, who is your life, appears, then you also will appear with him in glory" (Colossians 3:4). Here, Paul refers to a future event. Christmas arouses longing for the Parousia, the Second Coming. It awakens hope in that heralded upheaval, that upcoming earthquake that makes radical discipleship possible, ushering in as it will the ultimate fulfillment of human history.

Christian hope is neither Pollyanna optimism nor fragile wishful thinking that yields to discouragement and defeat. On the contrary, hope, a glimpse of the breakthrough for which Jesus stands, remains firm and serene in the face of terminal cancer.

Several years ago a priest visited a sixteen-year-old girl who lay dying in a Phoenix hospital. She looked into his worried and grief-stricken face, he recalls, and said to him, "Don't be afraid." This is the precise meaning of Christian hope: "Don't be afraid." It is most profound when the dying can say to the living, "Don't be afraid."[2]

Christian hope stands confident in the face of the Rome airport massacre, the turbulent Persian Gulf, the powder keg we call the Middle East, the agony of El Salvador, Honduras, Nicaragua. Hope remains unruffled by all the legalists, Puritans, Jansenists, party poopers and prophets of doom who have appeared on the scene since that memorable midnight when Mary spanked her baby and the infant Jesus screamed joy into a hushed and waiting world.

In the messianic cry, the Christmas contemplative discerns a sonorous, saving voice:

> Sshh! Be still. All is well. I am here. Do not be afraid. The world is no longer in the hands of the Evil One but in the arms of a loving Shepherd. In the end everything will be all right. Nothing can harm you permanently. No suffering is irrevocable, no loss is lasting; no defeat is more than transitory, no disappointment is conclusive. Nothing can ever separate us—not troubles, worries, persecutions, not lack of food or clothes, not attacks or invasions. There is absolutely nothing in life or death that will ever come between you and the love of God made visible before your eyes in this manger tonight.

Perhaps the only person in the church today who is more obnoxious than the prophet of doom is the prophet of joy. Yet the contemplative at Christmas, living one day at a time in a state of preparedness (in fact, homesickness) for the fullness of the Kingdom, listens intently as Paul tells the Philippians: "Rejoice in the Lord always. I will say it again: Rejoice! Let your gentleness be evident to all. The Lord is near. Do not be anxious about anything, but in everything, by prayer and petition, with thanksgiving, present your requests to God. And the peace of God, which transcends all understanding, will guard your hearts and your minds in Christ Jesus" (Philippians 4:4–7).

On an icy winter's night two weeks before Christmas 1977, I was at O'Hare Airport in Chicago.[3] All flights had been canceled due to fog and freezing rain. The airport terminal was in bedlam. Thousands of people were clustered at the ticket counters demanding a projected departure time; others were wrapped in stoic silence. Children were crying, the public address system was blaring and the defeated were bellying up to the bar. I was tense and apprehensive. I had to get to Texas to start a retreat the next day. How could the Gospel be preached in Dallas if the weather wouldn't shape up in Chicago?

Directly across from the plastic chair in which I slumped sat a middle-aged black woman with a child cradled in her arms. She was laughing. The world was collapsing, thousands were stranded, O'Hare was a shrieking snake pit and she was laughing! Irritated but also intrigued, I started watching her. She was rubbing her fingers across the child's lips, and he was blowing mightily: "Brhh. Brhh. Brhh."

She looked up and caught me staring.

"Ma'am," I said, "every other person here tonight is rattled and miserable. Would you mind telling me why you're so happy?"

"Sho," she said. "Christmas is coming and dat baby Jesus—He make me laugh."

I muttered something like "Oh." *Dat Jesus—He make me laugh!* I repeated it to myself. Hmm! Am I getting too serious about life? Have I let my sense of childlike wonder fade? Am I so caught up in preaching, teaching, writing and traveling that I no longer hear the sound of rain on the roof?

How long since I stopped making snowballs and flying kites? Am I growing uncomfortable with Jesus telling me to model my life after the birds and the flowers? Am I irritated with people, like this woman, who don't seem

183

to realize how serious life really is? Has getting serious about life meant becoming sad about life? Is living just another word for endurance?

Years ago in the seminary in Loretto, Pennsylvania, I was taught that the name Isaac (*Yishaq* in Hebrew) means laughter. Abraham and his wife Sarah had given up on God's promise of a child because of their advanced years. When Sarah was told that she would soon be pregnant, she laughed in disbelief. But God had the last laugh. A son was born to them in their old age, and the mirthless human laugh of despair turned into the Father's laughter of love. "They named their son 'Laughter' for he was a sign of the triumph of God's levity over man's gravity," writes theologian John Shea.

Isaac, son of the promise made to Abraham, was a prophetic foreshadowing of Jesus in whom the promise is fulfilled. Jesus is God's final laughter. Laughter is the celebration of incongruity, dissonance, lack of harmony. Nothing could be more incongruous in Hebrew tradition than a virgin having a baby.

Christmas is a faith experience that enables us to see beyond the tragic in our lives. It is a reminder that we need the laughter of God to prevent us from taking the world too seriously, the world of cerebral head trips played in dead earnest, the game of one-upmanship escalated to mortal combat, the illusions of self-importance. The Christian law of levity says that whatever falls into the earth will rise again. God's laughter is His loving act of salvation begun in Bethlehem, and Christian laughter is the echo of God's joy within us.

Christmas is the awesome mystery of the messianic Son of God in diapers. For the contemplative at Christmas it is "a glad tidings of great joy" that fills his heart with the laughter of the Father. "Now is your time of grief, but I will see you again and you will rejoice, and no one will take away your joy" (John 16:22).

184

I suspect that this is what my friend Carey Landry had in mind when he wrote that reverent and rollicking song, "And the Father Will Dance as on a Day of Joy."

As Advent draws to a close, go to the Father and ask Him, "Abba, why are You dancing?" See Him point to the manger and hear Him say, "Christmas is coming and dat baby Jesus—He make Me laugh!"

Christian hope, the spirit that dominates the Advent/ Christmas season, is not reserved merely for some splendid future yet to come. It is much more than an otherworldly matter, a promise of heavenly reward after death. Jesus does not ask us to wait until later, until the end for help and healing. Hope is the good news of transforming grace now. We are freed not only from the fear of death but from the fear of life; we are freed for a new life, a life that is trusting, hopeful and compassionate.

Unfortunately, the whole concept of grace is alien to the American psyche. In our culture the tradition of "rugged individualism" has assumed a religious dimension. Americans are the people par excellence who get things done. Give us enough time, money and manpower, and we can achieve anything. Listen to all the Sunday sermons with their emphasis on willpower and personal effort, and you get the impression that a do-it-yourself spirituality is the American fashion, that the Pelagian heresy is very much in vogue.

Though the Scriptures speak insistently of the divine initiative in the work of salvation, that by grace we are saved, that the Tremendous Lover has taken to the chase, American spirituality still seems to start with self, not with God. Personal responsibility replaces personal response. We seem engrossed in our own efforts to grow in holiness. We talk about acquiring virtue as if it were some kind of skill that can be acquired through personal effort, like good handwriting or a well-grooved golf swing. In seasons of penance, we focus on getting rid of our hangups and sweating through various spiritual experiences, as if they were a religious muscle-building program designed to produce that Christian Charles Atlas.

The emphasis is always on what I do rather than on what God is doing in my life. In this macho approach God is reduced to a benign old spectator on the sidelines. The American mystique orients us to attribute any growth in the spiritual life to our own sturdy efforts and vigorous resolutions. We become convinced that we can do a pretty good job of following Jesus if we just, once and for all, make up our minds and really buckle down to it. Well, if that's all there is to Christian discipleship, then in the words of singer Peggy Lee, "Let's break out the booze." All we're doing is transferring the Horatio Alger legend of the self-made man from the economic sphere to the spiritual one.

Yet we recite Psalm 123:2: "As the eyes of slaves look to the hand of their master, as the eyes of a maid look to the hand of her mistress, so our eyes look to the LORD our God." And we feel a vague existential guilt because our eyes are not on God but on ourselves. Or Psalm 130:6: "My soul waits for the Lord more than watchmen wait for the morning." We know this is no more than lip service. God really isn't that necessary; we can pull ourselves up to heaven by our own spiritual bootstraps.

Well, as each Advent begins, I am willing to wager that by December 15 we will be confronted with the utter inadequacy of our willpower, the total insufficiency of the self-made man. Then our security is shattered, our bootstrap myth blasted. We discover that we can't add a single inch to our spiritual stature. Any spirituality that furnishes a do-it-yourself kit plants the seeds of discouragement and disappointment. And this flowers into a winter of discontent that blooms in gloom, cynicism and a subtle form of despair.

186

There are three ways of committing suicide—taking my own life, letting myself die and *letting myself live without hope.* This last form of self-destruction is so subtle that it often goes unrecognized and therefore unchallenged. Ordinarily it takes the form of boredom, monotony, drudgery, feeling overcome by the ordinariness of life.

We begin by admitting in the inner sanctum of our hearts that the Christian calling is too demanding, that life in Christ Jesus is too sublime. We settle into a well-worn groove and lose the stuff of Gospel greatness. We become like everyone else, fail ourselves and the community by failing to respond to the living, vibrant, magnificent image of Christ that is within us waiting only to be expressed.

The spirituality of self-reliance is diametrically opposed to the Judeo-Christian tradition, which stresses the initiative of God in the work of our salvation. John writes: "This is love: not that we loved God, but that he loved us and sent his Son as an atoning sacrifice for our sins" (1 John 4:10). The contemplative at Christmas is not an autonomous self. All his aspirations of bearing fruit as a disciple are anchored in his personal relationship with Jesus Christ. His hope is Christ in person, because on Christmas day hope became incarnate.

We hear this Christmas hope in the voice of Daniel Berrigan. Sitting on the top tier of a bunk bed under a pale bulb in a jail cell in Washington, D.C., Berrigan scrawled notes in his journal. This man whose writing to me resembles that of William Faulkner, whose images burst the sentence structure, confesses, "I hardly have words, I am not capable of expressing how deeply, with all my heart, I believe in the words of Jesus, 'Do not fear . . . I am with you.'" Turning to his brother Phil he asks, "Can you imagine yourself apart from this promise?" Phil Berrigan says he cannot. Dan agrees: "Neither can I. It's almost like a game; watch me while I melt away, vaporize without Jesus; then describe me, the someone who was, the nothing that is."[4]

It is this "I am with you" that makes radical discipleship possible and livable. Jesus said: "Fear is useless; what is needed is trust. Don't live in fear, little flock; stop worrying, cheer up; be brave, take courage, have confidence in Me. I have conquered the world."

The spirituality of self-sufficiency, the attitude of "everything depends on me," bears no resemblance to the Gospel of Jesus Christ. Witnessing the multiplication of the loaves, the apostles were utterly and completely dumbfounded; their minds were closed to the power of the Spirit at work in Jesus to make the impossible possible.

The self-reliant rely on their own limited human resources. This is not the spirituality of Paul as he writes to the Ephesians: "I pray that our inward eyes may be illumined that you may realize how vast are the resources of his power open to us who believe in Him." The early Christians considered themselves supermen not because of superhuman willpower but because of reliance on the supernatural power of the Spirit.

The contemplative at Christmas is not timid, frightened or distraught at his lack of spiritual progress. Through his union with the Lord of his life, he is buoyed up and carried on by a life greater than his own.

The Christmas contemplative knows that hope is a gift, an undeserved gift of peace, but that it is also a call to decision—the decision to trust. One theologian says:

> Hope means that in Christ, by entrusting ourselves to him, we can courageously face evil, accept our own need for further conversion, the lovelessness of others and the whole legacy of sin around us and in our own past history. We can then face death later on just as we can face the mammoth task before us today, which, as Paul explains, "is putting to death our selfish desires."[5]

Hope thrives on the difficult and challenges the conclusion that our only contribution to the world will be, in the words of T. S. Eliot, "an asphalt driveway in front of our home and a thousand lost golfballs." Hope convinces us that in clinging to a miserable sense of security and status quo, the possibility of growth and greatness is utterly defeated. Hope says that I no longer need be dismayed over my personal dishonesty and self-centeredness and feeble life of faith, that I no longer need to feel defeated, insensitive and superficial.

Because the question no longer is: Can *I* do it? Am *I* able? Can *I* overcome my moodiness, my laziness, my sensuality, my grudges and my resentments? The only question is: Is Jesus Christ able? Can my Savior, the Lord of my life, revive my drooping spirit and transform *me* at Christmas as He transformed the world through His birth in Bethlehem?

There's no trace of defeat in Paul when, laboring under a mysterious affliction (whether a mental problem, an emotional hangup, a physical disability, a character defect—nobody really knows), he writes to the Corinthians:

> About this thing, I have pleaded with the Lord three times for it to leave me, but he has said, "My grace is enough for you: *my power is at its best in weakness.*" So I shall be very happy to make my weaknesses my special boast so that the power of Christ may stay over me, and that is why I am quite content with my weaknesses, and with insults, hardships, persecutions, and the agonies I go through for Christ's sake. For it is when I am weak that I am strong.
>
> 2 Corinthians 12:8–10 JB, italics added

I mentioned three ways of committing suicide: killing ourselves, letting ourselves die and *letting ourselves live without hope.* This is what Thoreau had in mind when

he wrote, "The mass of men live lives of quiet desperation." They still walk around. They still perform all the
gestures and movements that we identify as human.
But the fire inside of them has died. They have lost
the vision. They have lost what Boris Pasternak calls
"the inward music." They are zonked spectators carried
along on a mechanical sidewalk, like travelers at the
Atlanta airport.

When I was in bondage to booze, when I was lying in
the gutter on Commercial Boulevard in Fort Lauderdale, when every waking moment was dominated by
the desire for a drink, I knew myself to be one of these
living dead.

Do you relate at all to where I'm coming from? Has
despair ever destroyed all joy and courage in your life?
Has loneliness, unemployment, divorce, the loss of a
loved one, betrayal by a friend, a totally unforeseen
tragedy ever plunged you into similar darkness?

Or . . . is it the future, rather than anything in the
past, that casts the shadow on your life? The prophets
of doom today paint a paralyzing portrait of apocalyptic
disaster. We have no shortage of gloomy predictions and
forecasts. What we desperately need is a prophet of hope
with a vision of Good News. We are in urgent need of
a reason to go on. "Without a vision," says the book of
Proverbs, "the people perish" (29:18 KJV).

Where can we look for such a prophet, such a vision?
The contemplative at Christmas finds freedom from
fear, the courage to live as a lover, in the words of Paul
to the Colossians: "God has chosen to make known . . .
this mystery, which is Christ in you, the hope of glory"
(1:27).

"Christmas for the pagans is small publicity," G. K. Chesterton said; "for the Christian it is a gigantic secret."

And the gigantic Christmas secret is that Emmanuel,
God-with-us, is a baby boy "wrapped in swaddling clothes

190

and lying in a manger." When Jesus Christ is born in me, hope burns brightly and everything else fades into twilight. The roof can collapse, winter heat become unavailable, fair-weather friends shift their allegiance, popularity wane. The Kingdom of Christ Jesus remains alight within me. As Don Quixote tells Aldonza in *The Man of La Mancha:* "Wins and losses don't matter; all that matters is following the quest."

In the face of pessimistic appraisals that we have nothing going for us anymore, Christmas says that we have everything going—Jesus, the journey and the dream. Richard Roher says, "The Christian never loses, because he has nothing to lose."

My brothers and sisters in Christ Jesus, if you have been struck by the grace of Christmas, if the Lord in His mercy has given you the courage to accept acceptance, if you are convicted that Christmas is the decisive breakthrough of the passionate love of God in Jesus, if you trust that God is faithful to His promises, that He will finish what He began, that amazing grace is at work right now, that you have only checked into the hotel of earth overnight and you are en route to the heavenly Jerusalem, then in the immortal words of John Powell, "Please notify your face!"

On the other hand, if you have not been struck by the grace of Christmas, ask for it and it will be given. . . .

The golfer Arnold Palmer once played a series of exhibition matches in Saudi Arabia. The king was so impressed that he proposed to give Palmer a gift. Palmer demurred: "It really isn't necessary, Your Highness. I'm honored to have been invited."

"I would be deeply upset," replied the king, "if you would not allow me to give you a gift."

Palmer thought for a moment and said: "All right. How about a golf club? That would be a beautiful memento of my visit to your country."

The next day, delivered to Palmer's hotel was the *title* to a golf club. Thousands of acres, trees, lakes, clubhouse and so forth. . . .

The moral of this story is: In the presence of a king, don't ask for small gifts!

FOR REFLECTION

Begin with five minutes of silent prayer, becoming aware in faith of God's indwelling presence and humbly asking the Spirit to speak to your heart through Scripture, personal reflection and the insights of others.

Let one of the group read aloud Luke 11:1–13. Then focus on the following questions for personal reflection and group interaction.

1. Share with the group what was happening the last time you were struck by grace.
2. Do you experience difficulty in letting yourself be loved by God? Why?
3. If you have personally experienced Jesus Christ in your life, you qualify for the name tag "mystic," because the classic definition of mystic is a person who has experienced God. Shortly before his death in 1985, Karl Rahner prophesied, "In the days ahead, the Christian will either be a mystic or no Christian at all." Mystical experience is not a one-time thing. Do you agree or disagree with Rahner's statement? Are you comfortable with being called a mystic? Does your religious tradition use this term?

CHAPTER 13

Christmas Means Freedom

To Jesus' haunting question, "But who do you say that I am?" tumultuous events in my personal life in recent years have forged this reply: "You are the incarnation of the Father's freedom, the unfettered creative response to His love."

In choosing to be born in utter obscurity, the King of the universe ignored conventional expectations. He celebrated in His own birthday the freedom to be unorthodox. In failing to live up to people's presuppositions ("From Nazareth?" asks Nathanael. "Can anything good come from that place?"), Jesus became a stumbling block to many of His contemporaries. The housebroken Jewish imagination cringed at the crib, shuddered at the ersatz salvation of a humble, unpredictable God. A king in rags was an insult to the finely honed intellect of the Pharisee and the rational mind of the scribe. Simpleminded shepherds and the rabble who did not know the Law might be hoodwinked, but those who studied the Scriptures could not be deceived. There is a fascinating principle at work here in very religious people: "Messiah, You get our allegiance only when You fulfill our expectations."

Anthony DeMello tells that Bayazid, the Moslem holy man, sometimes acted deliberately against the outward forms and rituals of Islam. Once, on his way back from Mecca, he stopped at the Iranian town of Rey. The townsfolk, who revered him, rushed to make him welcome. Bayazid, who was tired of this adulation, waited till he reached the marketplace. There, although it was a day of fasting in the month of Ramadan, he bought a loaf of bread and began to munch it in full view of his admirers. The people of Rey were so scandalized at his behavior that they promptly deserted him. Bayazid remarked contentedly to a disciple, "Notice how the moment I did something contrary to their expectation, their veneration of me vanished."

Jesus scandalized His followers in similar ways. The multitudes need a saint to revere. The tacit contract is, however: "You must live up to our definition. The sanctity game!"[1]

In His public ministry, Jesus provoked opposition by His withering reappraisal of tradition and its representatives and by His freedom to break the Law when the love of persons demanded it.

The Law had become, at least for some, a means of self-justification, an instrument of social status and arrogant complacency. It had become a basis for moralistic judgments against others, a means of classifying and excluding them as sinners and apostates.

Instead of serving as a means of healing and building up the community, the law served as a tool for . . . establishing group hatred. Jesus is free to challenge such

194

use of law and repudiate it because he is also free for the law, the tradition and the past. He is free for the spirit of the law, for its essential meaning as a law of loving compassion and concern.[2]

Jesus was no maverick or renegade, but neither was He simplemindedly submissive to all the minutiae of the Law. The Law was made for persons, not persons for the Law (Mark 2:27). The Law exists for the humanization of men and women, not as an instrument of dehumanization. The Law is serviceable to the extent that it promotes the coming of the reign of God's love.

In making decisions, Jesus was called in freedom to ask first not what the Law says but what the Father would have Him do. A free life is often unconventional and surprising because it is available to those creative possibilities and innovative gestures that have been screened out of consideration by standards of acceptable behavior. In opting to celebrate His birthday in Bethlehem in such low-key fashion, Jesus revealed himself free from public opinion, from fear of what others might say or think. Jesus is the incarnation of the Father's freedom.

Paradoxically, while the freedom of Jesus is contagious for some, in others it arouses defensiveness. They have set their faces against freedom, against surprise, against novelty. The innovator must be suppressed in the name of Law, of tradition, of authority, of respectability, of good order—and a thousand other high-sounding phrases. "Any justification will suffice as long as the voice of judgment is silenced. For the free man is judgment against our own fear of freedom."[3]

Jesus came proclaiming a Gospel of freedom for captives. He invites and challenges His hearers, then and now, to enter the Kingdom of freedom, to be set free by His Father's love. The way of freedom is solitary and those who walk it are lonely. Scott Peck writes:

195

There are many who, by virtue of their passivity, dependency, fear and laziness, seek to be shown every inch of the way and have it demonstrated to them that each step will be safe and worth their while. This cannot be done. For the journey of spiritual growth requires courage and initiative and independence of thought and action. While the words of the prophets and the assistance of grace are available, the journey must still be traveled alone. No teacher can carry you there. There are no present formulas. Rituals are only learning aids, they are not the learning. . . . No words can be said, no teaching can be taught that will relieve spiritual travelers of picking their own ways, working out with effort and anxiety their own paths through the unique circumstances of their own lives toward the identification of their individual selves with God.[4]

In 1980 two Episcopal priests, Leo Frade and Joe Morris Doss, returned from Cuba with 437 Cuban refugees on a boat named *God's Mercy*. They were later convicted in U.S. District Court of violating the seldom-enforced "trading with the enemy" law. (Their convictions were overturned by the Appeals Court.) In a public defense of their boatlift rescue, Doss said:

Many people have accused us of having failed to be good priests, assuming that priests of the church should not be engaged in activities which would be judged criminal. It was assumed that we came to serve the good people of the church, to gather and pastor the flock, not to immerse ourselves in complex and controversial enterprises with foreign people.

But then, people have always misunderstood God's mission. For God's mission is always to call people out from a land of bondage into a land of freedom; to help people escape their own forms of slavery, whether it be oppression or laws or customs or prostitution or religious fetters or narrowmindedness or illusions or self-righteousness or any other enslaving force to which human beings fall victim; to help His people exodus into a land promised them.

Early in 1986, one of the most widely respected priests in the Roman Catholic archdiocese of Chicago announced he would defy the Vatican's ban on altar girls. In his parish newsletter, Father Leo Mahon, pastor of St. Victor Church in suburban Calumet City and leader of spiritual retreats through the archdiocese, described the Vatican's policy as "unfair and unjust to the point of cruelty." Mahon wrote:

> It may seem to some that this is a minor issue. After all, the world will not come to an end just because little girls are forbidden to serve Mass.
>
> But it is not a little matter. In fact, it is a gigantic issue. Behind this whole controversy is the question about the place of women in our world and in our church. Did God create women equal to men or not? If the answer to that question is yes, then any custom or practice which puts women in an inferior or secondary position is unfair, unjust and ultimately sinful. There is no doubt in my mind over whether God made us all equal. No matter what we may have said or done in the past, my conviction remains firm that we must hold woman to be the image of God just as much as man.
>
> If we of the church fail to hold and practice this, then we should be held responsible for discriminating against and disenfranchising half the human race. What an enormous rejection of God's design and plan.

After citing precedents for such dissent, Mahon urged that the issue be "opened to dialogue and, possibly, to reconsideration and reinterpretation. I believe that uncritical and universal acceptance of any authority—civic, religious or familial—makes mockery of obedience and leads, in the long run, to a rejection of authority itself."[5]

197

The church has always suffered from too many uncritical lovers and too many unloving critics. Some Christians have refused to ask any questions, while some nonbelievers seek to generate not light but heat. The authentic prophet walks the thin line between blind loyalty and death-dealing cynicism. The prophet is a living critic engaged in loyal dissent.

Unloving critics reject the presence of the Holy Spirit in the midst of human failure. Their anger consumes their hope. Confrontation is valid only if it is accompanied by a spirit of acceptance and faithfulness. If a prophet separates himself from the church (and by church I mean the whole Body of Christ), if a prophet separates himself from God's people, he can no longer lead them to hope; he can only join them in despair or withdraw into self-righteous isolation.

Beneath his fiery words there must be steadfast love and unflinching loyalty. Love is the power that transforms the anger of confrontation into the spirit of reconciliation.

Robert Frost once wrote:

> And were an epitaph to be my story
> I'd have a short one ready for my own.
> I would have written of me on my stone:
> I had a lover's quarrel with the world.

The Christian prophet is someone who has a lover's quarrel with the church. He is engaged in a struggle for hope, a conflict of love. His love is purified by truth, his criticism is tempered by loyalty. In any lover's quarrel there are no winners or losers—only the honest confrontation of conviction and the search for understanding. A lover's quarrel begins and ends in an atmosphere of fidelity. A prophet's struggle with his church is pursued with intensity, but it is grounded in faithfulness and permeated with love.[6]

I have found myself locked into a lover's quarrel with the Roman Catholic Church. The issue is a relatively minor one—the restoration of an ancient tradition, the married priesthood, which persevered until the year A.D. 1139. Dialogue has continued publicly and privately. Only time will prove where wisdom lies. Yet, with all the theological disagreement and deep emotion over matters of law, structure, tradition and authority, I can say with that wise, witty and Spirit-filled old Jesuit Walter Burkhardt:

> I love this church, this living, pulsing, sinning People of God, with a crucifying passion. Why? For all the Christian hate, I experience here a community of love. For all the institutional idiocy, I find here a tradition of reason. For all the individual repression, I breathe here an air of freedom. For all the fear of sex, I discover here the redemption of my body. In an age so inhuman, I touch here tears of compassion. In a world so grim and humorless I share here rich joy and earthy laughter. In the midst of death, I hear an incomparable stress on life. For all the apparent absence of God, I sense here the real presence of Christ.[7]

To be faithful is to know who we are and to speak that word in season and out, delivered from mindless fidelity to "movements," which ignore the fact that going with the drift leads the church away from its Gospel moorings, which become so institutionalized that the voice of freedom and fraternal correction is silenced.

Only a small minority of Christians preserve a sense of themselves as they journey into adulthood. That coherent sense of self endows them with wisdom and compassion and, in the words of Daniel Berrigan, "the capacity to create a countercurrent to the drift."

For this little band of Christians, Christmas is more than a theological concept. Concepts do not cry for their mother's milk. Christmas is the revelation of God's freedom. Jesus is the countercurrent to the drift of messianic expectations of a triumphant king.

Yves Congar points out that,

> the revelation of Jesus is not contained in his teaching alone; it is also, and perhaps we ought to say mainly, in what he *did*. The coming down of the Word into our flesh, God's acceptance of the status of a servant, the washing of the disciples' feet—all this has the force of a revelation and a revelation of God.[8]

The incarnation of the Father's freedom calls us beyond admiration to transformation. A recent convert to Jesus was approached by an unbelieving friend: "So you have been converted to Christ?"

"Yes."

"Then you must know a great deal about Him. Tell me, what country was He born in?"

"I don't know."

"What was His age when He died?"

"I don't know."

"How many sermons did He preach?"

"I don't know."

"You certainly know very little for a man who claims to be converted to Christ."

"You are right. I am ashamed at how little I know about Him. But this much I know: Three years ago I was a drunkard. I was in debt. My family was falling to pieces; they dreaded the sight of me. But now I have given up drink. We are out of debt. Ours is a happy home. My children eagerly wait my return home each evening. All this Christ has done for me. This much I know of Christ!"

To know is to be transformed by what one knows.

To ape the ways of the world in celebrating Christmas is to go with the drift. To mimic secular standards of a good time is to lose our sense of self. To be intimidated by the cultural patterns of the landlocked, dues-paying, lockstepping, product-consuming majority is the declaration of our unfreedom. To be seduced from following our path and letting the expectations of others act as a subtle but controlling pressure on our Advent preparation and Christmas celebration is people-pleasing enthrallment.

Jesus calls us at Christmas to enter into the Kingdom of Liberty, to be set free by His Father's love. There is a refreshing quality about the Nazarene without whom Christianity would never have become a fact of history. The surprise of His birth in Bethlehem fires a longing to be free from self and free for others. It sparks a search for intelligent and imaginative ways to celebrate an unconventional Christmas.

The wailing Infant bears witness to a God whose Word is fresh and alive, who is not the defender of the old, the already-settled, the well-established and familiar. The God we encounter in Jesus is free from preoccupation with His own glory, free to be for us, free to be gracious, free to love and let be.

This Christmas such a God might well expect us to be creatively responsive and thus truly Christlike. Indeed, He might call us to set free captives bound by loneliness and isolation, to share our hope with prisoners of gloom and despair, to invite the unlovely to our table, to celebrate our freedom in forgetfulness about our comfort and convenience, to cry the Gospel by ministering to widows and orphans, to be the church by bringing soup to the poor, to ignore conventional expectations, to call His Son out of Egypt once more.

FOR REFLECTION

Begin with five minutes of silent prayer, becoming aware in faith of God's indwelling presence and humbly asking the Spirit to speak to your heart through Scripture, personal reflection and the insights of others.

Let one of the group read aloud 2 Corinthians 3:16 and Galatians 6:1. Then focus on the following questions for personal reflection and group interaction.

1. Recall and share a time when you acted counter-culturally, ignored conventional wisdom and disappointed purposely the expectations of family and friends. Were you scared? Why?
2. If your conscience urged you to take a position on abortion, homosexuality or another controversial moral issue contrary to the normative, evangelical teaching, what would you do?
3. How do you understand these words: "A free person is judgment against our own fear of freedom"? Why is there so much unfreedom in religious circles today?

CHAPTER 14

The Shipwrecked at the Stable

D o you think you could contain Niagara Falls in a teacup?

Is there anyone in our midst who pretends to understand the awesome love in the heart of the Abba of Jesus that inspired, motivated and brought about Christmas? The shipwrecked at the stable kneel in the presence of mystery.

God entered into our world not with the crushing impact of unbearable glory but in the way of weakness, vulnerability and need. On a wintry night in an obscure cave, the infant Jesus was a humble, naked, helpless God who allowed us to get close to him.

We all know how difficult it is to receive anything from someone who has all the answers, who is completely cool, utterly unafraid, needing nothing and in control of every situation. We feel unnecessary, unrelated to this paragon. So God comes as a newborn baby, giving us a chance to love Him, making us feel that we have something to give Him.

The world does not understand vulnerability. Neediness is rejected as incompetence and compassion is dismissed as unprofitable. The great deception of television advertising is that being poor, vulnerable and weak is unattractive. A fat monk named "Brother Dominic" is cute and cool because he conquers vulnerability and helplessness by buying into the competitive world with a Xerox copy machine.

The spirituality of Bethlehem is simply incomprehensible to the advertising industry. As Matthew Fox says: "The opening notes of Beethoven's Fifth Symphony are being used to sell us pain reliever and the prayer of St. Francis is being used to sell us hair conditioner."

The Bethlehem mystery will ever be a scandal to aspiring disciples who seek a triumphant Savior and a prosperity Gospel. The infant Jesus was born in unimpressive circumstances; no one can say exactly where. His parents were of no social significance whatsoever, and His chosen welcoming committee were all turkeys, losers and dirt-poor shepherds. But in this weakness and poverty the shipwrecked at the stable would come to know the love of God.

Sadly, Christian piety down the centuries has prettified the Babe of Bethlehem. Christian art has trivialized divine scandal into gingerbread crèches. Christian worship has sentimentalized the smells of the stable into dignified pageant. (And some not so dignified. Years ago I was in a parish in Pittsburgh on Christmas Eve. At midnight a statue of the infant came sliding down a long cylindrical laundry chute and plopped into the crib directly in front of the high altar. In the background I thought I heard the voice of Ed McMahon shouting, "And heeeeeere's Jesus!")

204

Pious imagination and nostalgic music rob Christmas of its shock value, while some scholars reduce the crib to a tame theological symbol. But the shipwrecked at the stable tremble in adoration of the Christ child and quake at the inbreaking of God Almighty, because all the Santa Clauses and red-nosed reindeer, fifty-foot trees and thundering church bells put together create less pandemonium than the infant Jesus when, instead of remaining a statue in a crib, He comes alive and delivers us over to the fire that He came to light.

The Spanish author José Ortega puts it this way:

> The man with the clear head is the man who frees himself from fantasy and looks life in the face, realizes that everything in it is problematic, and feels himself lost. And this is the simple truth—that to live is to feel oneself lost. Whoever accepts this has already begun to find himself, to be on firm ground. *Instinctively, as do the shipwrecked,* he will look around for something to which to cling, and that tragic ruthless glance, absolutely sincere because it is a question of his salvation, will cause him to bring order into the chaos of his life. *These are the only genuine ideas; the ideas of the shipwrecked.* All the rest is rhetoric, posturing, farce. He who does not really feel himself lost is without remission; that is to say, he never finds himself, never comes up against his own reality.[1]

The shipwrecked at the stable are the poor in spirit who feel lost in the cosmos, adrift on an open sea, clinging with a life-and-death grip to one solitary plank. Finally, they are washed ashore and make their way to the stable, stripped of the old spirit of possessiveness in regard to anything. The shipwrecked find it not only tacky but utterly absurd to be caught up either in tinsel trees or in religious experiences—"Doesn't going to church on Christmas make you feel good?" They are not concerned with their own emotional security or any

205

of the trinkets of creation. They have been saved, rescued, delivered from the waters of death, set free for a new shot at life. At the stable in a blinding moment of truth, they make the stunning discovery that Jesus is the plank of salvation they have been clinging to without knowing it!

All the time they were battered by wind and rain, buffeted by raging seas, they were being held even when they didn't know who was holding them. Their exposure to spiritual, emotional and physical deprivation has weaned them from themselves and made them reexamine all they once thought important. The shipwrecked come to the stable seeking not to possess but to be possessed, wanting not peace or a religious high but Jesus Christ.

The shipwrecked don't seek peace because they aren't disturbed by the lack of it. By that I mean the subjective feeling of peace. Circumstances can play havoc with our emotions. The day can be stormy or fair and our feelings will fluctuate accordingly, but if we are in Christ Jesus, we are in peace and therefore unflustered *even when we feel no peace.* Meister Eckhart's equation "In Christ equals in peace" is always valid. When we accept the truth of ourselves—shipwrecked and saved—our lives are henceforth anchored in the Rock who is Christ, not in the shifting sands of our fickle feelings.

This is a point of capital importance for those who would fully experience the grace of Christmas. When we are in right relationship with Jesus, we are in the peace of Christ. Except for grave, conscious, deliberate infidelity, which must be recognized and repented of, the presence or absence of *feelings* of peace is the normal ebb and flow of the spiritual life. When things are plain and ordinary, when we live on the plateaus and in the valleys (which is where most of the Christian life takes place) and not on the mountaintops of peak religious experiences, this is no reason to blame ourselves, to think that our relationship with God is collapsing or to echo Magdalene's cry in the garden, "Where has my beloved gone?" Frustration, irritation, fatigue and so forth may temporarily unsettle us, but they cannot rob us of living in the peace of Christ Jesus. As the playwright Ionesco once declared in the middle of a depression: "Nothing discourages me, not even discouragement."

The shipwrecked have stood at the still-point of a turning world and discovered that the human heart is made for Jesus Christ and cannot really be content with less. They cannot take seriously the demands that the world makes on them. During Advent they teach us that the more we try to tame and reduce our desires, the more we deceive and distort ourselves. We are made for Christ, and nothing less will ever satisfy us. As Paul writes in Colossians 1:16, "All things were created by him and for him." And further on, "There is only Christ: he is everything" (3:11 JB). It is only in Christ that the heart finds true joy in created things.

To the clotheshorse fretting about what to wear on Christmas Day, the shipwrecked say, "Put on Christ." To the merchant whose Bible is the *Wall Street Journal* and who pants down the money-making street, the shipwrecked say, "You have only one Master; serving Him is incompatible with any other servitude." To the power broker dealing from strength to get things done, the shipwrecked say, "However powerful you are, the most you can do is change the decor of a world that is collapsing into its own death."

The shipwrecked stand on firm ground. They live in truth and are rooted in reality. They do not allow the world to order them around. Kneeling at the curb they find the vanity of the world ridiculous, bloated, preposterous. Amused at the pretentiousness of kings, presidents, rock stars and conglomerates, they sing the Christmas carol written by St. Ephrem:

Come, Jesus, rest and keep quiet in your mother's
   lap. . . .
What sort of baby are you, so merry and bright?
Beautiful child! Your mother is chaste and your Fa-
   ther the Hidden One whom not even angels can see.
What sort of being are you?
Tell us, O son of the merciful.
Feuding enemies who came to look at you became
   merry and bright; they laughed together and were
   at one with each other.
Angry men became sweetened through you and your
   gentleness.
Who are you, child, that even what is sour becomes
   sweet through you?
Whoever saw a baby so eager to meet all who are near
   him?
Tucked up in his mother's lap
He reached out even to those who are far off.
What a beautiful sight, this child whose whole concern
   is with everyman, that they all should see him.
Some came and saw you, bowed down with their
   cares, and their cares fled away.
And the brooder who came forgot all his brooding.
And the hungry forgot, because of you, even his food.
And men at the errands, seduced by you, forgot where
   they were going.
Quiet yourself down, child, and leave us men
To get on with our business.[2]

Do you hear what the shipwrecked are saying? Let
go of your paltry desires and expand your expectations.
Christmas means that God has given us nothing less than
Himself, and His name is Jesus Christ. Be unwilling next
Christmas to settle for anything else. Don't order "just a
piece of toast" when eggs Benedict are on the menu. Don't
come with a thimble when God has nothing less to give
you than the ocean of Himself. Don't be contented with
a "nice" Christmas when Jesus says, "It has pleased My

Father to give you the Kingdom." Pray, go to work, play Trivial Pursuit, eat banana bread, exchange presents, go caroling, feed the hungry, comfort the lonely and do all in the name of our Lord Jesus Christ.

A beautiful story is recounted every Christmas in the forest of Provence in southern France. It's about the four shepherds who came to Bethlehem to see the child. One brought eggs, another brought bread and cheese, the third brought wine. And the fourth brought nothing at all. People called him "L'Enchanté." The first three shepherds chatted with Mary and Joseph, commenting how well Mary looked, how cozy was the cave and how handsomely Joseph had appointed it, what a beautiful starlit night it was. They congratulated the proud parents, presented them with their gifts and assured them that if they needed anything else, they had only to ask. Finally, someone asked, "Where is L'Enchanté?" They searched high and low, up and down, inside and out. Finally, someone peeked through the blanket hung against the draft, into the crèche. There, kneeling at the crib, was L'Enchanté—the Enchanted One. Like a flag or a flame taking the direction of the wind, he had taken the direction of love. Through the entire night, he stayed in adoration, whispering, "Jesu, Jesu, Jesu—Jesus, Jesus, Jesus."

As Christmas approaches, an honest question is: Do I want to be or merely *appear* to be a Christian? Like the shipwrecked, the Enchanted One is laid waste by one pure passion. His singlemindedness leads him to a realistic assessment: Anything connected with Christmas that is not centered in Christ Jesus—tree, ornaments, turkey dinner, exchange of gifts, worship itself, is empty gesturing. Blessed are the shipwrecked, for they see God in all the trappings of Christmas and experience a joy that the world does not understand.

One day Saint Francis and Brother Leo were walking down the road. Noticing that Leo was depressed, Francis turned and asked, "Leo, do you know what it means to be pure of heart?"

"Of course. It means to have no sins, faults or weaknesses to reproach myself for."

"Ah," said Francis, "now I understand why you're sad. We will always have something to reproach ourselves for."

"Right," said Leo. "That's why I despair of ever arriving at purity of heart."

"Leo, listen carefully to me. Don't be so preoccupied with the purity of your heart. Turn and look at Jesus. Admire Him. Rejoice that He is what He is—your Brother, your Friend, your Lord and Savior. That, little brother, is what it means to be pure of heart. And once you've turned to Jesus, don't turn back and look at yourself. Don't wonder where you stand with Him.

"The sadness of not being perfect, the discovery that you really are sinful, is a feeling much too human, even borders on idolatry. Focus your vision outside yourself on the beauty, graciousness and compassion of Jesus Christ. The pure of heart praise Him from sunrise to sundown. Even when they feel broken, feeble, distracted, insecure and uncertain, they are able to release it into His peace. A heart like that is stripped and filled—stripped of self and filled with the fullness of God. It is enough that Jesus is Lord."

After a long pause, Leo said, "Still, Francis, the Lord demands our effort and fidelity."

"No doubt about that," replied Francis. "But holiness is not a personal achievement. It's an emptiness you discover in yourself. Instead of resenting it, you accept it and it becomes the free space where the Lord can create anew. To cry out, 'You alone are the Holy One, you alone are the Lord,' that is what it means to be pure of heart. And it doesn't come by your Herculean efforts and threadbare resolutions."

"Then how?" asked Leo.

"Simply hoard nothing of yourself; sweep the house clean. Sweep out even the attic, even the nagging, painful consciousness of your past. Accept being shipwrecked. Renounce everything that is heavy, even the weight of your sins. See only the compassion, the infinite patience and the tender love of Christ. Jesus is Lord. That suffices. Your guilt and reproach disappear into the nothingness of nonattention. You are no longer aware of yourself, like the sparrow aloft and free in the azure sky. Even the desire for holiness is transformed into a pure and simple desire for Jesus."

Leo listened gravely as he walked along beside Francis. Step by step he felt his heart grow lighter as a profound peace flooded his soul.

The shipwrecked have little in common with the landlocked. The landlocked have their own security system, a home base, credentials and credit cards, storehouses and barns, their self-interest and investments intact. They never find themselves because they never really feel themselves lost. At Christmas, one despairs of finding a suitable gift for the landlocked. "They're so hard to shop for; they have everything they need."

The shipwrecked, on the contrary, reach out for that passing plank with the desperation of the drowning. Adrift on an angry sea, in a state of utter helplessness and vulnerability, the shipwrecked never asked what they could *do* to merit the plank and inherit the kingdom of dry land. They knew that there was absolutely nothing any of them could do. Like little children they simply *received* the plank as a gift. And little children are precisely those who haven't done anything. "Unless you . . . become like little children, you will never enter the kingdom of heaven" (Matthew 18:3). Jesus is not suggesting that heaven is a vast playground for infants. Children are our model because they have no claim on heaven. If they are close to God, Simon Tugwell says, "it is not because they are innocent, but because they are incompetent."[3]

For the shipwrecked, "becoming a little child" means accepting oneself as being of little account. If a little Jewish child received a ten-cent allowance from her father at the end of the week, she never regarded it as payment or reward for sweeping the house or going to the store; it was a wholly unmerited gift, a gesture of her father's liberality.

When Jesus tells us to become like little children, He is urging us to forget what lies behind. Children have no past. Whatever we have done in the past, be it good or evil, great or small, it is irrelevant to our stance before Jesus. It is only *now* that we are in His presence, and this Christmas is the first Christmas of the rest of our lives. Like little children the shipwrecked don't bring the baggage of the past into the stable of the present moment.

One summer day we went to the beach in Biloxi, Mississippi. Our little daughter Nicole went skipping into the Gulf of Mexico and immediately found a five-dollar bill floating on the water. Bursting with joy, she raced back to tell us and everybody else between Biloxi and Pensacola Beach, Florida, of her splendid find. She was radiant. She needed nothing else to be happy.

Jesus says: "The kingdom of heaven is like treasure hidden in a field. When a man found it, he hid it again, and then in his joy went and sold all he had and bought that field. Again, the kingdom of heaven is like a merchant looking for fine pearls. When he found one of great value, he went away and sold everything he had and bought it" (Matthew 13:44–46).

Both stories focus on the element of joy in the discovery of the Kingdom. The one who finds the treasure bubbles all the way to the real estate office because he knows what a splendid find he has come upon. The pearl merchant realizes that the pearl-of-great-value is worth far more than what is being asked for it. Even if he has to sell everything he possesses to buy it, it is easily worth the cost. He knows he has stumbled on an extraordinarily profitable transaction and rejoices at the thought of the payoff.

Scripture scholar Joachim Jeremias says:

When that great joy, surpassing all measure, *seizes* a man, it carries him away, penetrates his inmost being, subjugates his mind. All else seems valueless compared with that surpassing worth. No price is too great to pay. The unreserved surrender of what is most valuable becomes a matter of course. The decisive thing in the twin parables is not what the two men give up, but their reason for doing so—the overwhelming experience of the splendor of their discovery. Thus it is with the kingdom of God. The effect of the joyful news is overpowering; it fills the heart with gladness; it changes the whole direction of one's life and produces the most wholehearted self-sacrifice.[4]

The shipwrecked at the stable are captivated by joy and wonder. They have found the treasure in the field of Bethlehem. The pearl of great price is wrapped in swaddling clothes and lying in a manger. Everything else is cheap, fake, painted fragments of glass.

The question for all of us is what we will really aim at next Christmas. If all we are going for is a placid decency, routine prayer, well-behaved worship and comfortable compassion, then we have effectively parted company with the shipwrecked and have no fellowship with the pearl finder.

I wonder, if we were to stop people at random in the street on December 24th and ask them what they want most for Christmas, how many would say, "I want to see Jesus"?

I believe that the single most important consideration during the sacred season of Advent is *intensity of desire.* Paraphrasing the late Rabbi Abraham Heschel, "Jesus Christ is of no importance unless he is of supreme importance." An intense inner desire is already the sign of His presence in our hearts. The rest is the work of the Holy Spirit.

Perhaps many of us are in the same position as the Greeks in chapter 12 of John's Gospel who approached Philip and said, "We would like to see Jesus."

The question addressed to each of us is: How badly?

The shipwrecked at the stable are an indispensable presence in the church. They rescue the Savior from the snares of convention and the clutches of organized religion. They are marginal men and women, not leaders or decision makers. In their ministry of quiet presence they do not need to win or compete. They may look like losers even to themselves. If they courted the world, the world might respect them; if they rejected the world in sullen disdain, it might respect them even more. But because they take notice at all of what the world thinks of them, they are mocked and made fun of.

The only explanation of why the little band of the shipwrecked exists at all is the personal magnetism of Jesus. As Bernard of Clairvaux wrote, "Only he who has experienced it can believe what the love of Jesus Christ is." You could more easily catch a hurricane in a shrimp net than you can understand the wild, relentless, passionate, uncompromising, pursuing love of God made present in the manger.

In 1980, the day before Christmas, Richard Ballenger's mother in Anderson, South Carolina, was busy wrapping packages and asked her young son to shine her shoes. Soon, with the proud smile that only a seven-year-old

214

can muster, he presented the shoes for inspection. His mother was so pleased that she gave him a quarter.

On Christmas morning as she put on the shoes to go to church, she noticed a lump in one shoe. She took it off and found a quarter wrapped in paper. Written on the paper in a children's scrawl were the words, "I done it for love."

When the final curtain falls, each of us will be the sum of our choices throughout life, the sum of the appointments we kept and the appointments we didn't keep. The glory of the shipwrecked will be that they habitually failed to turn up for duty. In their defense they claim they were detained by a baby in swaddling clothes. When interrogated as to why they hung out at the stable, they answer, "We done it for love."

In their integrity the shipwrecked preserve the meaning of Christmas in its pristine purity—the birthday of the Savior and the eruption of the messianic era into history.

This Christmas, may you belong to their number.

FOR REFLECTION

Begin with five minutes of silent prayer, becoming aware in faith of God's indwelling presence and humbly asking the Spirit to speak to your heart through Scripture, personal reflection and the insights of others.

Let one of the group read aloud John 20:19–21. Then focus on the following questions for personal reflection and group interaction.

1. From your own experience have you found that you can be at peace even when you feel no peace?
2. Tell about your last experience of shipwreck and the feelings that accompanied it.

3. When was the last time you heard Jesus say, "It gives joy to My heart that you love Me. It delights Me." Close your eyes, pause a while, become still and listen. You have read *The Relentless Tenderness of Jesus* and met together faithfully for these fourteen weeks with but one purpose in mind—to come to a more intimate, heartfelt understanding of Jesus as Lord, Savior, Brother and Friend. As you listen, can you hear Jesus saying these words to you now, "It gives joy to My heart to know that you love Me. It delights Me"?

Stand, join hands, pray the Lord's Prayer together and embrace one another with the sign of peace.

Notes

Chapter 1 Healing Our Image of God and Ourselves

1. James Burtschaell, *Philemon's Problem: The Daily Dilemma of the Christian* (Chicago: The ACTA Foundation, 1973), 21.
2. Ibid., 20.
3. Dick Westley, *Redemptive Intimacy* (Mystic, Conn.: Twenty-third Publications, 1981), 136.

Chapter 2 The Day I Met Jesus

1. Sean Caulfield, *The Experience of Praying* (Ramsey, N.J.: Paulist Press, 1980), 67.

Chapter 4 The Affluent Poor

1. William E. Reiser, *Into the Needle's Eye—Becoming Poor and Hopeful under the Care of a Gracious God* (Notre Dame, Ind.: Ave Maria Press, 1984), 53.
2. Ibid., 55.
3. Carroll Stuhlmuller, *The Prophets and the Word of God* (Notre Dame, Ind.: Fides Press), 224.

Chapter 5 Showdown in the Spirit

1. Jim Wallis, *The Call to Conversion* (New York: Harper and Row, 1981), 30, 34.
2. C. S. Lewis, *Mere Christianity* (New York: Macmillan, 1952), 56.
3. Mary Craig, *Blessings* (New York: William Morrow, 1979), 124.
4. Ibid., 120.

Chapter 6 The Transparent Disciple

1. Dorothy L. Sayers, quoted in *The Jesus Book,* comp. and ed. Michael E. McCauley (Chicago: Thomas More Publishing, 1978), 210.
2. Sebastian Moore, *The Inner Loneliness* (New York: Crossroad, 1982), 85.

Chapter 7 Living Out of the Center

1. Robert Gleason, *Christ and the Christian* (New York: Sheed and Ward, 1960), 12.
2. Ibid., 18.
3. The substance of this reflection is drawn from Peter van Breeman's *Called by Name* (Denville, N.J.: Dimension Books, 1980), 53.
4. Peter van Breeman, *Certain as the Dawn* (Denville, N.J.: Dimension Books, 1980), 37.
5. Donald Gray, *Jesus, the Way to Freedom* (Winona, Minn.: St. Mary's Press, 1979), 47.

Chapter 9 Lion and Lamb: The Relentless Tenderness of Jesus

1. Henri Nouwen, *Compassion, A Reflection on the Christian Life* (Garden City, N.Y.: Doubleday), 24.
2. Ibid., 30.

3. Walter Burkhardt, *Tell the Next Generation* (Ramsey, N.J.: Paulist Press, 1982), 80.

4. Nouwen, *Compassion,* 30.

5. Thomas Merton, quoted by Burkhardt, *Tell the Next Generation,* 192.

6. Laurens Van der Post, quoted in *Caring* by Morton Kelsey (Ramsey, N.J.: Paulist Press), 96.

7. James Shannon, quoted by Burkhardt, *Tell the Next Generation,* 14.

8. Kelsey, *Caring,* 23–24.

9. Henri Nouwen, *Here and Now* (New York: Crossroad, 1994), 101.

Chapter 10 The Great Season of Hope

1. van Breeman, *Certain as the Dawn,* 13.

Chapter 11 The Crisis of Christmas

1. Albert Nolan, *Jesus Before Christianity* (Maryknoll, N.Y.: Orbis Books, 1978), 135–36.

2. William MacNamara, *Mystical Passion* (Chicago: Claretian Press, 1978), 58.

Chapter 12 The Contemplative at Christmas

1. Paul Tillich, *The Shaking of the Foundations* (New York: Charles Scribner's Sons, 1948), 161–62.

2. Burkhardt, *Tell the Next Generation,* 210.

3. Brennan Manning, *Souvenirs of Solitude* (Denville, N.J.: Dimension Books, 1979), 35–37. This section was previously published in a chapter entitled "Christmas Reflection at O'Hare."

4. John Heagle, *A Contemporary Meditation on Hope* (Chicago: Thomas More Publishing, 1976), 18.

5. Bernard Haring, *A Sacramental Spirituality* (St. Louis, Mo.: Herder and Herder, 1972), 112.

Chapter 13 Christmas Means Freedom

1. Anthony deMello, *The Song of the Bird* (Chicago: Loyola University Press, 1982).
2. Gray, *Jesus, the Way to Freedom,* 46.
3. Ibid., 49.
4. M. Scott Peck, *The Road Less Traveled* (New York: Simon and Schuster, 1979), 311.
5. John McKenzie, *Source* (Chicago: Thomas More Publishing, 1984), 206.
6. Heagle, *Contemporary Meditation,* 124.
7. Burkhardt, *Tell the Next Generation,* 114.
8. Avery Dulles, *Models of Revelation* (Garden City, N.Y.: Doubleday, 1983), 161.

Chapter 14 The Shipwrecked at the Stable

1. José Ortega, *The Revolt of the Masses* (New York: Norton, 1957), 157.
2. Simon Tugwell, *The Beatitudes: Soundings in Christian Traditions* (Springfield, Ill.: Templegate, 1985), 127–28.
3. Ibid., 6.
4. Joachim Jeremias, *The Parables of Jesus* (New York: Charles Scribner's Sons, 1970), 84.

Brennan Manning leads spiritual retreats for people of all ages and backgrounds around the world most every week of the year. He's written thirteen books and has been featured in five videos recorded from his speeches and retreats. His best-selling book *The Ragamuffin Gospel* has inspired new and old generations and moved the late singer/songwriter Rich Mullins to name his band The Ragamuffins.

Manning combines his training as a former Franciscan priest and college professor with his knowledge of the street. He grew up in Brooklyn, New York, in the post-Depression era; attended St. John's University in Queens; served the U.S. Marine Corps overseas in the Korean War; and studied journalism at the University of Missouri before a "restless search" led him to a Catholic seminary in Loretto, Pennsylvania. He studied there and graduated St. Francis College after four years of advance studies in theology, philosophy and Latin.

He was ordained to the Franciscan priesthood in May 1963 and served several poor communities throughout Europe and the U.S. He also served as campus minister at the University of Steubenville and liturgy instructor and spiritual director at St. Francis Seminary, and was a graduate student in creative writing at Columbia University and in Scripture and liturgy at Catholic University of America.

In the late 1960s he joined the Little Brothers of Jesus of Charles de Foucauld, an order committed to an un-cloistered, contemplative life among the poor—spending days in manual labor and nights in silence and prayer. He became a dishwasher in France, aguador (transporting water to rural villages via donkey and buckboard) and mason's assistant (shoveling mud and straw) in Spain, voluntary prisoner in a Swiss jail (his identity as a priest known only to the warden), and spent periods of solitude in a remote cave in the Zaragoza desert.

Back in the U.S. in the seventies, Manning and four other priests established an experimental community of home and church among the shrimp boat workers on the Mississippi Bay in the bustling seaport city of Bayou La Batre, Alabama.

Manning resumed campus ministry in the late seventies at Broward Community College, Ft. Lauderdale, Florida —a successful ministry interrupted by a precipitate col-lapse into alcoholism. He began writing books during his recovery and after six months of treatment, culminating at the Hazelden treatment center in Minnesota.

He left the Franciscan Order in the eighties and settled in New Orleans, where he makes his home, when not traveling, today.

For more information on his ministry and spiritual retreats, visit www.brennanmanning.com or write to Willie Juan Ministries, P.O. Box 6911, New Orleans, LA 70114.